Be Anxious for Nothing

Be Anxious for Nothing

A Biblical Guide to Overcoming Anxiety

Sean Ewing

RESOURCE *Publications* • Eugene, Oregon

Resource Publications
An Imprint of Wipf and Stock Publishers
199 W. 8th Ave., Suite 3
Eugene, OR 97401

www.wipfandstock.com

PAPERBACK ISBN: 979-8-3852-4974-9
HARDCOVER ISBN: 979-8-3852-4975-6
EBOOK ISBN: 979-8-3852-4976-3

VERSION NUMBER 04/21/25

Contents

Introduction

ANXIETY IS A UNIVERSAL human experience. It creeps into our minds uninvited, tightening its grip around our thoughts, distorting reality, and whispering fears that feel all too real. It's the heaviness that keeps us awake at night, the racing heart in moments of uncertainty, the overwhelming sense that things are slipping beyond our control. No one is immune—young or old, new believers or seasoned followers of Christ. Anxiety touches everyone at some point, yet its grip doesn't have to define us.

The world offers many solutions to anxiety, meditation, self-help techniques, distraction, or even avoidance. But none of these can truly address the heart of the issue from a biblical perspective. The Bible presents a different response, one that doesn't dismiss anxiety or minimize its effects, but instead offers a lasting path to peace rooted in God. Scripture speaks directly to the anxious heart, providing not only comfort but also a clear and practical way to navigate the storm. The invitation is clear "Do not be anxious about anything, but in every situation, by prayer and petition, with thanksgiving, present your requests to God. And the peace of God, which transcends all understanding, will guard your hearts and your minds in Christ Jesus" (Philippians 4:6–7).

This book is an invitation to experience that peace, not as a fleeting feeling, but as an anchored reality in Christ. It's not a promise that anxiety will vanish overnight or that struggles will never return. Rather, it's a call to walk in the truth of God's Word, to bring every fear before him, and to rest in the security of his sovereignty.

Throughout these chapters, we will explore anxiety from a biblical perspective, what it is, where it comes from, and how God provides a way through it. We will examine the roots of anxiety, uncover how distorted views of God affect our struggles, and see how lament can be a pathway to peace. We will learn how prayer is more than a recitation of requests but a surrender to God's control, and how the finished work of Christ offers the ultimate foundation for true rest. The journey will be both theological and practical, addressing not only what Scripture teaches but also how to live it out daily. We will also emphasize the importance of seeking support from fellow believers and qualified counselors when needed, recognizing that God often uses others to minister to us in our struggles.

This book doesn't promise quick fixes or shallow reassurances. Instead, it offers a deeper reality, one where faith replaces fear, truth overcomes lies, and God's presence becomes the ultimate refuge in moments of distress. The path to overcoming anxiety is not found in human strength but in dependence on the One who holds all things together.

Anxiety may be a universal struggle, but God's peace is a universal invitation.

I

Anxiety and the Bible

A Foundational Understanding

ANXIETY IS A COMMON struggle, touching nearly everyone at some point. It can manifest as persistent worry, fear of the unknown, or distress over circumstances beyond our control. From a biblical perspective, anxiety isn't simply an emotional response; it's a spiritual issue revealing where we place our trust. The Bible acknowledges the reality of anxiety but doesn't suggest managing it through human strength alone. Instead, Scripture encourages believers to bring their fears to God, trusting in his sovereignty, care, and provision.

Anxiety often stems from uncertainty about the future. In Matthew 6:25–34, Jesus directly addresses this, cautioning against anxious thoughts about daily needs. He reminds his followers that their heavenly Father knows their needs and calls them to prioritize his kingdom above worrying about tomorrow. This passage highlights that anxiety arises when our focus shifts from God's faithfulness to our perceived inability to control events.

The Bible consistently contrasts two responses to anxiety, a fear-driven response leading to doubt and misplaced trust in human strength, and a faith-driven response calling believers to

1

depend on and obey God. Philippians 4:6–7 instructs, "Do not be anxious about anything, but in every situation, by prayer and petition, with thanksgiving, present your requests to God. And the peace of God, which transcends all understanding, will guard your hearts and your minds in Christ Jesus." The solution to anxiety isn't self-reliance but entrusting every burden to the Lord.

Throughout Scripture, God's people faced overwhelming situations that could have caused deep distress. David, pursued by enemies, poured out his fears to the Lord but found confidence in God's deliverance (Psalm 56:3–4). Elijah, after a great victory over the prophets of Baal, fled in fear, but God met him in his distress and reminded him of his sovereign presence (1 Kings 19:9–13). Paul, facing imprisonment and suffering, anchored his hope in Christ and encouraged others to do the same (2 Corinthians 1:8–10). These examples illustrate that anxiety isn't a new struggle but one consistently met with God's faithfulness.

Understanding anxiety biblically means recognizing it as an opportunity to deepen our trust in God. It's not something to accept passively but a battle to be fought with truth, prayer, and obedience. As Isaiah reminds us, "You will keep in perfect peace those whose minds are steadfast, because they trust in you" (Isaiah 26:3). The path to peace isn't through human effort but through steadfast reliance on God's unchanging character and promises.

UNDERSTANDING VIGILANCE VS. ANXIETY

Anxiety can feel inescapable, but Scripture distinguishes between fear that enslaves and concern that reflects godly wisdom. Not all caution or awareness of danger constitutes sinful anxiety. The Bible calls believers to be discerning and alert, not to live in constant fear. Understanding the difference between vigilance and anxiety is key to responding to life's uncertainties in a way that honors God.

Vigilance is a readiness to respond to challenges with faith and wisdom. Proverbs 27:12 states, "The prudent see danger and take refuge, but the simple keep going and pay the penalty." Godly vigilance acknowledges reality, prepares wisely, and trusts in

God's sovereignty, not reacting with fear. Nehemiah exemplified vigilance when rebuilding the walls of Jerusalem. He prayed, made strategic plans, and remained watchful for threats (Nehemiah 4:9). His response stemmed from trust in God's provision while acting responsibly, not from anxiety.

Anxiety, from a biblical perspective, is more than mere worry—it is a spiritual struggle marked by a consuming focus on potential negative outcomes. At its heart, anxiety reveals a deeper issue, a wavering trust in God's sovereign care and an underlying desire to control circumstances ourselves, rather than surrendering them to his wisdom and power. Scripture consistently portrays anxiety as a symptom of spiritual unrest, signaling areas in our hearts where we have yet to fully embrace the truth of God's unchanging character and promises. Unlike vigilance, which prompts action based on faith, anxiety can lead to paralysis, excessive worry, or fruitless striving. Jesus warns against this kind of fearful thinking in Matthew 6:27, asking, "Can any one of you by worrying add a single hour to your life?" Anxiety doesn't produce wisdom or protection; it drains strength and distracts from trust in God.

The crucial difference between vigilance and anxiety lies in where we place our trust. Vigilance prepares but rests in God's control, while anxiety fixates on uncertainty and assumes the burden of securing every outcome. One operates from faith, the other from fear. As we explore anxiety from a biblical perspective, remember that God calls his people to wise preparation, never to a life ruled by anxious thoughts. Biblical counseling helps individuals discern the root of their anxiety and cultivate a reliance on God's peace, transforming anxious thoughts into faithful action.

A BIBLICAL CASE STUDY MARTHA'S WORRY AND JESUS' RESPONSE (LUKE 10:38–42)

Anxiety often creeps into our daily lives and entangling itself with responsibilities, expectations, and unspoken pressures. It whispers that everything hinges on our efforts, that life will fall apart if we don't maintain absolute control. This is not a modern phenomenon; it's a timeless human experience. Scripture offers profound insights into the heart of anxiety, guiding us from turmoil toward trust in God. One of the most illuminating examples of this comes from the encounter between Jesus and two sisters, Mary and Martha, in Luke 10:38–42.

MARTHA'S ANXIETY, A DIVIDED HEART

"As Jesus and his disciples were on their way, he came to a village where a woman named Martha opened her home to him. She had a sister called Mary, who sat at the Lord's feet listening to what he said. But Martha was distracted by all the preparations that had to be made. She came to him and asked, 'Lord, don't you care that my sister has left me to do the work by myself? Tell her to help me!' 'Martha, Martha,' the Lord answered, 'you are worried and upset about many things, but few things are needed—or indeed only one. Mary has chosen what is better, and it will not be taken away from her.'" (Luke 10:38–42)

Martha is introduced as a hospitable woman, eager to serve and ensure everything is in order as she welcomes Jesus into her home. Her intentions are good—she wants to honor her guest through her work. However, in the process, she becomes overwhelmed, pulled in multiple directions by tasks, expectations, and the weight of responsibility. Her heart is divided, caught between her desire to serve and the deeper need to simply be present with Jesus. This moment offers a clear picture of anxiety—when the mind is restless, consumed with endless to-dos, unable to find peace. Martha's struggle is not just about busyness; it is about misplaced priorities. She is doing good work, but in her striving, she is missing the most important thing—being with Christ.

THE REMEDY FOR WORRY

Like many of us when overwhelmed, Martha attempts to regain control of the situation. She approaches Jesus, requesting that he intervene and instruct Mary to assist her. However, Jesus' response is not one of condemnation; instead, he speaks with gentle compassion "Martha, Martha, you are worried and upset about many things" (v. 41). By repeating her name, he conveys deep care and concern, highlighting the burden she carries.

Jesus identifies the root issue, Martha is anxious and troubled about many things, but only one thing is truly necessary. Mary has chosen that one thing, to sit at Jesus' feet and listen to his words. In this moment, Jesus redefines true priorities. It's not the flawless execution of service or the completion of every task, but a heart that prioritizes him above all else.

LESSONS FROM MARTHA'S EXPERIENCE

Martha's story offers several key insights into anxiety and how we can respond to it:

1. Anxiety is often linked to distraction—Like Martha, we can become consumed with numerous things, even good things, and lose sight of what is most important, our relationship with God. Our hearts and minds become divided, leading to inner turmoil.

2. Jesus invites us to refocus on what truly matters—Instead of allowing anxiety to dictate our actions, we are invited to sit at his feet, to trust him, and to listen to his guidance.

3. Serving is valuable, but being with Jesus is more valuable—Martha's desire to serve was not inherently wrong, but her priorities were misaligned. Service should flow from a heart of worship, not from a burden of worry.

4. Jesus cares deeply about our anxious hearts—his response to Martha was not one of frustration, but of compassion. He calls her name, acknowledging her struggle, and offers a better way, resting in him.

CHOOSING THE "ONE THING"

Mary's choice to sit at Jesus' feet embodies a posture of trust and surrender to God. Anxiety often flourishes when we believe that everything depends on us and our abilities. But Jesus gently reminds us that only one thing is needed, to be near him, to listen, and to trust that he is in control. When we shift our focus from anxious striving to abiding in Christ, we begin to experience the peace that he offers.

The invitation remains open will we, like Martha, remain consumed by many things? Or will we, like Mary, choose what is better? Jesus' words to Martha echo through time, offering us a new way to respond to anxiety, not with control, but with trust in God. Only one thing is truly needed, to draw near to Christ and let him calm our anxious hearts.

GRACE FOR THE ANXIOUS SOUL

It's important to speak gently to those already burdened by anxiety. While anxiety can reveal the posture of our hearts, it isn't always the result of intentional wrongdoing. Sometimes, anxiety is a natural response to living in a difficult world, intensified by weakness, exhaustion, or deep sorrow. Scripture never diminishes our pain, and neither does our compassionate God. He understands our limitations. He is not only our King but also our gentle Shepherd, who gathers the broken and carries them close. If you begin this study feeling weary or ashamed, remember that Jesus welcomes you. You are not condemned in your weakness; you are invited to rest in God who is strong enough to carry your soul and your sorrows. This book encourages deeper trust, not harder effort. Look to God who knows, understands, and lovingly draws near.

CHAPTER SUMMARY

Anxiety is a universal human experience that touches all lives, regardless of age or spiritual maturity. The Bible doesn't ignore anxiety; instead, it offers a way through it, calling believers to bring their worries before God rather than carrying them alone. This chapter examines anxiety from a biblical perspective, recognizing that it reveals where we place our trust. Jesus' teaching in Matthew 6:25–34 emphasizes that anxiety stems from misplaced focus worrying about the future rather than trusting in God's provision.

Through the biblical case study of Martha and Mary (Luke 10:38–42), we see how Martha's anxiety was fueled by distraction and misplaced priorities. Her divided heart led her to focus on her responsibilities rather than on Christ himself. Jesus gently corrected her, reminding her that only one thing is truly needed, a heart that seeks him above all else. This passage teaches that while responsibilities and vigilance are necessary, they should never take precedence over resting in God's presence. Anxiety diminishes when our trust is anchored in God's sovereignty, not in our ability to control outcomes.

Scripture provides a consistent contrast between two responses to anxiety, fear-driven striving versus faith-driven surrender. Figures like David, Elijah, and Paul faced overwhelming situations but found peace by entrusting themselves to God. The key to overcoming anxiety is not self-reliance but embracing the peace that comes from depending on Christ. Philippians 4:6–7 assures that prayer, thanksgiving, and surrender lead to a peace that transcends understanding, guarding our hearts and minds.

Ultimately, this chapter invites believers to shift their perspective from anxiety to trust, from fear to faith, and from striving to abiding in Christ. The goal is not merely to manage anxiety but to cultivate a deeper dependence on God, allowing his presence to be the ultimate refuge in times of distress.

HOMEWORK ASSIGNMENTS

Reflective Questions

1. What earthly things do you tend to rely on when you feel anxious, and how do they fall short of true peace?

2. How does understanding the brokenness of the world through Genesis 3 change the way you view your anxious thoughts?

Identifying Anxiety Triggers and Redirecting Focus

Over the next three days, be mindful of moments when anxiety surfaces. Write down what triggered your anxiety, the thoughts running through your mind, how your body responded, and how you reacted. After identifying patterns, turn to prayer using Philippians 4:6–7 as a guide. Instead of dwelling on worry, choose to pray and replace anxious thoughts with God's promises. Practice gratitude by writing down three things you're thankful for each day.

Practicing Rest in God's Presence

For the next five days, set aside 15–20 minutes daily to be intentionally with God. Choose one or more ways to connect with him, such as reading and meditating on a short Psalm (like Psalm 23, 46, or 91), listening to worship music, sitting in quiet reflection, or writing down what you sense God is speaking to your heart through Scripture. At the end of the week, reflect on how this practice affected your anxiety, what distractions tried to pull you away, and what you learned about God's presence and peace.

These practices are designed to help you anchor your heart in Christ rather than be consumed by anxiety. Let each step draw you closer to God's steady and comforting presence.

2

The Roots of Anxiety

Understanding the Causes

As we've seen, anxiety isn't simply a modern struggle; it has been part of human experience since sin entered the world. Jesus' interaction with Martha revealed how anxiety divides our hearts and distracts us from what is most important. But to fully understand anxiety, we must delve deeper. Why do we experience it? What is at its root? And how does the Bible explain its presence in our lives?

Scripture teaches that anxiety is not just a circumstantial issue but a deeply spiritual one, rooted in the brokenness of a fallen world. To truly address anxiety biblically, we must begin at the beginning where sin first entered the human story.

ANXIETY IN A FALLEN WORLD
(GENESIS 3, ROMANS 8:18–25)

Anxiety was not part of God's original design for creation. In the Garden of Eden, Adam and Eve lived in perfect fellowship with God. There was no fear, no uncertainty, only peace, trust, and joy in the presence of their Creator. But when sin entered the world through their disobedience, everything changed.

Genesis 3 describes this tragic turning point. Adam and Eve, once unashamed before God and each other, immediately felt fear and shame after they sinned. They hid from God instead of walking freely with him (Genesis 3:8). When confronted, Adam shifted blame instead of taking responsibility (Genesis 3:12). Eve, too, attempted to justify her actions (Genesis 3:13). The consequences of sin extended beyond them—pain, toil, broken relationships, and ultimately, death (Genesis 3:16–19).

Anxiety is a byproduct of this fall. It is the natural result of separation from God and the brokenness of a world no longer aligned with his perfect order. Before sin, Adam and Eve had no reason to worry. Their needs were provided for, their relationships were whole, and they lived in the security of God's presence. But after sin entered the world, fear, insecurity, and self-preservation took hold of the human heart.

This fallen condition isn't just an ancient reality; it is the backdrop of every human struggle with anxiety today. The fear of being exposed, the worry of being abandoned, the relentless striving to control outcomes—all of these trace back to the Garden, where mankind first chose independence from God over trust in him.

Romans 8:18–25 expands on this reality, describing the ongoing effects of sin on creation itself "The creation waits in eager expectation for the children of God to be revealed" (v. 19). The world is not as it should be. It longs for restoration, for redemption, for the return of the peace that was lost in the Fall. "The creation was subjected to frustration, not by its own choice, but by the will of the one who subjected it" (v. 20). Sin has fractured the world, our bodies, our minds, our relationships; even nature itself groans under the weight of its effects. "We know that the whole creation has been groaning as in the pains of childbirth right up to the present time" (v. 22). Anxiety, suffering, and sorrow are all part of this groaning. "But if we hope for what we do not yet have, we wait for it patiently" (v. 25). There is hope, an assurance that redemption is coming and that God is in the process of restoring all things.

These passages teach us that anxiety exists because we live in a world that is not yet fully redeemed. Until Christ returns and makes all things new, we will continue to feel the effects of sin, including fear, uncertainty, and anxiety. However, Scripture also assures us that this is not the end of the story. While anxiety is a natural result of the Fall, it is not meant to control or define us. Christ came to restore what was lost, and through him, we can experience the firstfruits of peace even now, as we wait for the fullness of redemption.

APPLYING THIS TRUTH TO OUR LIVES

Understanding anxiety through the reality of a fallen world offers two important benefits. First, it alleviates the guilt and shame often linked to this struggle. Many Christians mistakenly believe anxiety indicates a lack of faith or personal failing. However, the Bible shows us that anxiety is part of the broader brokenness caused by sin's impact on creation, not simply a personal flaw. Recognizing this truth allows us to approach anxiety biblically—with compassion instead of shame, and with hope in God's redeeming grace.

Second, this perspective shifts our focus toward God's ultimate plan. If we see anxiety only as a temporary emotional problem, we'll seek temporary fixes. But understanding its deeper spiritual roots allows us to address anxiety as Scripture directs—not by trying to control our circumstances, but by grounding our hope in the sovereign God who promises to restore everything. While the effects of sin and brokenness are undeniable, God's redemption is far greater than our anxieties.

With this understanding as our foundation, let's explore different types of anxiety—situational, chronic, and spiritual—and discover how Scripture uniquely speaks to each.

TYPES OF ANXIETY

Anxiety manifests differently for each person, varying in intensity, frequency, and cause. Some experience it fleetingly, while others face a daily struggle. The Bible addresses these different forms of anxiety, offering wisdom and guidance for each. To better understand anxiety from a biblical perspective, we will examine three primary types, situational anxiety, chronic anxiety, and spiritual anxiety.

SITUATIONAL ANXIETY A NATURAL RESPONSE TO LIFE'S UNCERTAINTIES

Situational anxiety isn't inherently sinful; it's a normal human reaction, even seen in Christ himself in the Garden of Gethsemane (Luke 22:44). However, the difference lies in where we take that anxiety, do we let it consume us, or do we surrender it to God? Philippians 4:6–7 calls believers to bring every worry before God with thanksgiving, trusting that his peace will guard our hearts. When faced with situational anxiety, the biblical response isn't self-reliance but surrender to God's sovereignty.

BIBLICAL RESPONSE TO SITUATIONAL ANXIETY

When you feel anxious, remember that God cares deeply about your fears and wants you to bring them to him honestly. You don't have to manage worry alone. He invites you to cry out to him, promising to listen with compassion (Psalm 34:4). When life feels overwhelming, remind yourself that the same Jesus who calmed the storm (Matthew 8:23–27) has power over your situation too. Instead of letting fear control you, God lovingly invites you to trust in his presence, promises, and strength (Isaiah 41:10). As you shift your focus to him, you'll find peace that goes beyond the anxious moment, grounded in his faithful and tender care.

CHRONIC ANXIETY

Unlike situational anxiety, chronic anxiety is a persistent struggle that often lacks a clear trigger. It's an ongoing sense of worry, fear, or unease that lingers even when life seems stable. This can show up as constant restlessness, difficulty trusting God's provision, and a tendency to imagine the worst. Martha's story in Luke 10:38–42 illustrates this well. She was "worried and upset about many things," revealing a deeper, ongoing struggle, not just a fleeting concern.

Chronic anxiety often stems from a life focused on personal control rather than trust in God, trying to manage every detail instead of resting in his care. But Jesus offers a compassionate invitation to those burdened by this anxiety "Come to me, all you who are weary and burdened, and I will give you rest . . . For my yoke is easy and my burden is light" (Matthew 11:28–30).

Ultimately, chronic anxiety is more than just an emotion; it's a deeply spiritual issue. It reflects an ongoing battle to fully trust God. Therefore, Scripture encourages us to continuously renew our minds with truth (Romans 12:2) and intentionally capture every anxious thought, bringing it into obedience to Christ (2 Corinthians 10:5).

BIBLICAL RESPONSE TO CHRONIC ANXIETY

Responding biblically to chronic anxiety starts with acknowledging the deeply personal and overwhelming nature of this struggle. God invites you into a daily rhythm of rest and renewal in him, gently urging you to fill your mind and heart regularly with his comforting Word (Psalm 119:165). Instead of carrying tomorrow's burdens today, he encourages you to intentionally surrender your worries each day, trusting in his faithful care (Matthew 6:34). When anxious thoughts arise—and they will—remember that God patiently meets you there. He helps you gently but deliberately redirect those thoughts toward his reassuring truths (2 Corinthians 10:5). As you consistently practice this, you'll experience Christ's compassionate presence transforming your anxieties into peace.

SPIRITUAL ANXIETY, THE BURDEN
OF A TROUBLED SOUL

Spiritual anxiety often stems from a sensitive heart grappling with uncertainty, doubt, or guilt in its relationship with God. It can manifest as a persistent fear of judgment or rejection (1 John 4:18), a quiet worry about truly belonging to him (Romans 8:15–16), or a painful sense of God's distance (Psalm 13:1–2). King David exemplified this struggle. After his sin with Bathsheba, he cried out in Psalm 51:11, "Do not cast me from your presence or take your Holy Spirit from me." David's anxiety reveals the profound distress we feel when our connection with God seems broken, often due to our own sin and brokenness.

However, spiritual anxiety isn't always a sign of personal failing. Even devoted believers experience seasons of doubt and spiritual distance. God understands these struggles and tenderly assures us of his nearness, especially when we feel heartbroken or overwhelmed (Psalm 34:18). Scripture lovingly reminds us that nothing—no fear, doubt, or perceived distance—can separate us from God's love (Romans 8:38–39). Our security rests on Christ's work, not our own efforts (Ephesians 2:8–9).

While the enemy uses spiritual anxiety to push us away from God, the Bible encourages us to approach him boldly, trusting in his mercy and grace (Hebrews 4:16). He welcomes us in our anxiety and weakness, gently comforting our hearts and drawing us close.

BIBLICAL RESPONSE TO SPIRITUAL ANXIETY

When spiritual anxiety burdens your heart, find comfort in Jesus' unwavering promise, nothing can separate you from his secure love (John 10:28–29). Rest confidently in this truth, knowing your salvation is eternally safe in him. If you feel that unaddressed sin is creating distance or worry, come to God with humble honesty. He lovingly promises not only to forgive you but also to cleanse your heart completely (1 John 1:9). Remind yourself daily of the gospel's comforting core Christ's sacrifice is fully sufficient and forever complete. You don't need to carry the weight of wondering if you measure up. Through faith in Christ, you have a peace with God that no circumstance can undo (Romans 5:1).

APPLYING THESE TRUTHS

Identifying the type of anxiety we experience allows us to apply biblical wisdom more effectively. Scripture offers guidance tailored to situational, chronic, or spiritual anxiety, providing a clear path forward. The first step involves discerning the root of our anxiety, whether it arises from a temporary circumstance, a persistent burden, or a struggle in our faith. Once we understand the source, we are called to bring it to God in prayer, drawing near to him rather than allowing fear to pull us away.

Regardless of the cause, the biblical response to anxiety is surrender before the Lord, trusting in his care. Furthermore, replacing anxious thoughts with biblical truth is essential. God's Word serves as both a weapon against fear and the foundation for lasting peace, reminding us of his faithfulness and sovereignty.

While anxiety is an unavoidable part of life in a fallen world, it does not need to control our hearts. Through Christ, we have access to a peace that surpasses understanding, a peace that is not dependent on our circumstances but firmly rooted in who God is and his faithfulness.

SELF-RELIANCE VS. TRUST IN GOD

At the heart of anxiety lies a fundamental question, whom do we trust, ourselves or God? Anxiety often reveals a lack of belief in who God is and his word, along with our desire to control circumstances, outcomes, and the future. It subtly whispers that we must rely on our strength, our plans, and our abilities to manage life's uncertainties. However, Scripture consistently warns against this self-reliant posture, urging us instead to anchor our trust firmly in God's character, sovereignty, and faithfulness.

Proverbs 3:5–6 clearly instructs us "Trust in the Lord with all your heart and lean not on your own understanding; in all your ways submit to him, and he will make your paths straight." Here, the Bible draws a direct contrast between self-reliance ("leaning on your own understanding") and trust in God. Leaning on ourselves is exhausting; it demands constant attention, fuels anxiety, and places the entire burden of outcomes squarely on our shoulders. Trusting in God, however, shifts our dependence from finite human strength to his infinite wisdom and power. The result is not merely emotional relief but spiritual freedom.

Self-reliance often disguises itself as responsible living, saying things like, "If I don't take care of this, no one else will," or, "Everything depends on me." While responsibility and stewardship are biblical virtues, they must always flow from a posture of trust rather than a fear-driven effort to control outcomes. The Bible repeatedly shows how self-reliance creates anxiety, whereas trust in God brings peace. Psalm 127:1–2 powerfully illustrates this truth "Unless the Lord builds the house, the builders labor in vain. Unless the Lord watches over the city, the guards stand watch in vain. In vain you rise early and stay up late, toiling for food to eat—for he grants sleep to those he loves."

The message is clear, self-reliance results in anxious striving and ultimately proves futile. God-reliance, on the other hand, provides rest even amid uncertainty. This does not imply passivity or irresponsibility. Rather, it emphasizes active dependence on God—taking wise, faithful steps but leaving the outcomes securely in his hands.

In Matthew 6:25–34, Jesus repeatedly emphasizes this same principle. He points to birds and flowers, neither of which anxiously strive, yet both receive abundant care from God. He concludes "But seek first his kingdom and his righteousness, and all these things will be given to you as well. Therefore, do not worry about tomorrow, for tomorrow will worry about itself" (Matthew 6:33–34). Jesus' words remind us that anxiety flourishes where self-reliance dominates, but peace grows from trust in God's care.

RECOGNIZING ANXIETY TRIGGERS

The struggle between self-reliance and trusting God begins with a gentle examination of your heart. What anxieties specifically stir within you? Anxiety is personal; what unsettles one person may not affect another. Perhaps it's uncertainty about the future—finances, health, or relationships. Or maybe it's the fear of failure or rejection in your work, ministry, or personal life. Unexpected events and feeling out of control can also trigger overwhelming fear. The pressures we face, whether self-imposed, societal, or from others, can lead to self-doubt.

God understands these struggles and we see example in Scripture. It offers examples of people who faced similar anxieties, sometimes relying on their own strength and sometimes trusting in God's faithfulness. Recognizing your personal anxiety triggers empowers you to intentionally choose trust over fear. Instead of reacting from a place of self and limited strength, you can proactively respond with God's truth and care.

Abraham experienced anxiety regarding the fulfillment of God's promises and attempted to solve matters through his own wisdom (Genesis 16:1–6). His self-reliance created complications, yet God faithfully fulfilled his promise despite Abraham's anxious striving.

Peter faced anxiety when walking on the water toward Jesus (Matthew 14:28–31). As soon as he shifted his gaze from Christ to the waves, his anxiety increased, and he began sinking. Peter's experience teaches that anxiety grows as we focus more on our circumstances and less on the presence and power of Jesus.

Recognizing anxiety triggers from a biblical perspective means asking ourselves, when do I feel most anxious? Identifying specific situations or thoughts that spark anxiety helps reveal areas where self-reliance may dominate. What am I believing in those moments? Anxiety often arises from believing lies—that everything depends on me, that God is distant, or that I must control outcomes. Scripture calls us to identify these lies and replace them with God's truth (Romans 12:2). Am I responding with prayer or my own efforts? Philippians 4:6–7 emphasizes prayerful surrender as the biblical response to anxiety. If our immediate response is more effort or control, it indicates we're relying on ourselves rather than God.

David models how recognizing triggers leads to deeper trust in God. In Psalm 139:23–24, he prays "Search me, God, and know my heart; test me and know my anxious thoughts. See if there is any offensive way in me, and lead me in the way everlasting." David knew that identifying anxiety triggers was critical to walking in trust. His prayer encourages us to invite God to search our hearts, reveal hidden anxieties, and lead us into deeper dependence on him.

APPLYING THESE TRUTHS TO OUR LIVES

Understanding the battle between self-reliance and trust in God, as well as identifying personal anxiety triggers, is foundational to overcoming anxiety biblically. One of the first steps in this process is cultivating self-awareness through prayerful reflection. Regularly asking God to reveal where self-reliance rules the heart and inviting him to expose specific situations or thought patterns that trigger anxiety allows for intentional surrender of those areas to him. Additionally, countering anxious thoughts with biblical truth is crucial. When anxiety begins to rise, it is important to actively confront the underlying lies by recalling Scripture that affirms God's control, care, and promises. Jesus' words in John 14:27 serve as a reminder of the peace he offers "Peace I leave with you; my peace I give you. I do not give to you as the world gives. Do not let your hearts be troubled and do not be afraid." Finally, replacing self-reliant striving with prayerful dependence shifts the burden from personal effort to God's sovereignty. Instead of attempting to manage outcomes alone, believers are called to entrust every worry to God's wisdom and care, as Psalm 56:3 encourages "When I am afraid, I put my trust in you." While anxiety will never fully disappear in a fallen world, its power diminishes significantly when we recognize our triggers, surrender our self-reliance, and rest in the unwavering security of our sovereign and loving God.

CHAPTER SUMMARY

This chapter delves into the underlying causes of anxiety from a biblical perspective. Anxiety entered human experience as a direct consequence of sin in the Garden of Eden (Genesis 3). Before the Fall, humanity enjoyed perfect fellowship with God, living securely, free from fear and worry. However, the brokenness introduced by sin made anxiety a universal human struggle, a reflection of our fractured relationship with God and the uncertainties of a fallen world (Romans 8:18–25).

We identified three primary expressions of anxiety, situational, chronic, and spiritual. Situational anxiety arises temporarily in response to specific events or stressors. Chronic anxiety is persistent, often rooted in a desire for control and self-reliance. Spiritual anxiety stems from a troubled relationship with God, characterized by doubts, guilt, or fear of rejection.

A key to understanding anxiety lies in recognizing the contrast between self-reliance and trust in God. Anxiety often reveals where we've misplaced our trust in ourselves rather than God. Scripture calls us away from anxious striving and toward deep dependence on God's character and sovereignty (Proverbs 3:5–6). This dependence is foundational to experiencing lasting peace and freedom from anxiety.

Finally, we explored the importance of identifying personal anxiety triggers—specific situations or thoughts that consistently stir anxiety in our hearts. By recognizing these triggers and intentionally surrendering them to God through prayer and the truth of Scripture, we can begin to experience the profound peace that comes from trusting in him rather than relying on ourselves. This active surrender is a practical step toward managing anxiety and cultivating a deeper reliance on God's provision and care.

HOMEWORK ASSIGNMENTS

Reflective Questions

1. What earthly things do you tend to rely on when you feel anxious, and how do they fall short of true peace?
2. How does understanding the different types of anxiety change the way you view your anxious thoughts?

Identifying Your Anxiety Type

Review the definitions of situational anxiety, chronic anxiety, and spiritual anxiety. Reflect on which type or combination you experience most often. Write in your journal about specific examples from your life that fit each type. Include at least two Bible verses from the chapter that speak to your situation and write a personal prayer, asking God to help you rest in his truth despite your anxiety.

Recognizing and Responding to Anxiety Triggers

Throughout the week, pay attention to moments of anxiety and jot them down in your journal. Note what triggered the anxiety and how you responded. Once you identify a pattern, go back to Proverbs 3:5–6 and consider how you could respond differently next time. At the end of the week, reflect on any patterns you notice and write down one practical step you will take to practice trusting God rather than relying on your own strength.

3

Finding Peace in Lament

Overcoming Anxiety Through Biblical Expression

UNDERSTANDING THE ROOTS OF anxiety helps us see that it's not simply a fleeting emotion but a deeply spiritual struggle tied to the brokenness of this world and what we believe in our heart about God. We've seen how anxiety manifests in different forms, situational, chronic, or spiritual, and how self-reliance fuels its grip on our hearts. The biblical response is always to shift our trust from ourselves to God, surrendering every fear into his sovereign hands. But what does that surrender look like? How do we move from acknowledging our anxiety to truly experiencing God's peace?

One of the most powerful, yet often overlooked, biblical tools for overcoming anxiety is lament. Scripture doesn't call us to suppress our fears, nor does it demand that we put on a false front of unwavering strength. Instead, God invites us to bring our burdens before him with honesty, wrestling through our emotions in a way that ultimately leads to trust. This is the practice of biblical lament, a deeply personal and transformative way of processing anxiety through faith.

WHAT IS BIBLICAL LAMENT?

Lament is more than sorrow or complaint; it's a sacred expression of trust in the midst of suffering. Throughout Scripture, lament is the language of the weary, the brokenhearted, and the anxious. It's the cry of those who feel overwhelmed yet refuse to turn away from God. Unlike grumbling, which doubts God's goodness, lament clings to the truth of who he is, even when circumstances seem unbearable.

The Bible is filled with examples of lament, particularly in the Psalms. Nearly one-third of the Psalms contain lament, where the writers pour out their distress before the Lord. Psalm 42 and Psalm 77 illustrate this beautifully, both begin with deep anguish and uncertainty, yet they don't end there. Lament isn't about staying in sorrow; it's a process that moves the anxious heart toward trust.

At its core, biblical lament follows a pattern, crying out to God, remembering his faithfulness, surrendering in trust, and ultimately praising him. It's the bridge between fear and faith, between anxiety and peace. In the next section, we'll explore how lament can transform our response to anxiety, guiding us from restless worry to confident trust in the God who hears, cares, and redeems.

HOW LAMENT TRANSFORMS ANXIETY INTO TRUST (PSALM 42, PSALM 77)

Anxiety thrives in isolation. When we keep our fears locked inside, they grow louder, distorting our perception of reality and making God feel distant. Biblical lament offers a way forward—not by ignoring our struggles, but by honestly bringing them before God. Lament transforms anxiety into trust by allowing us to express our deepest fears and uncertainties while anchoring us in the unchanging character of God. Psalm 42 and Psalm 77 provide powerful examples of how lament moves the anxious heart from despair to faith.

PSALM 42 WRESTLING WITH
DESPAIR, LONGING FOR GOD

Psalm 42 begins with an aching cry "As the deer pants for streams of water, so my soul pants for you, my God. My soul thirsts for God, for the living God. When can I go and meet with God?" (Psalm 42:1–2).

The psalmist is spiritually dry, longing for the presence of God, yet feeling distant from him. This is a common experience for those battling anxiety, feeling as though God is absent, as though peace is just out of reach. The psalmist acknowledges his pain "My tears have been my food day and night, while people say to me all day long, 'Where is your God?'" (Psalm 42:3).

Yet, even in this despair, he doesn't turn away from God. Instead, he speaks truth to himself "Why, my soul, are you downcast? Why so disturbed within me? Put your hope in God, for I will yet praise him, my Savior and my God" (Psalm 42:5).

This is the turning point of lament, rather than allowing anxiety to dictate his thoughts, the psalmist preaches to his own soul. He acknowledges his pain, but he refuses to let it define him. He directs his heart back to trust, reminding himself that God is still worthy of praise, even when his emotions say otherwise.

This shift in focus is critical. Anxiety often magnifies our fears and minimizes God's presence. Lament counters this by reorienting our hearts toward truth, even when we don't feel it. The psalmist repeats this refrain twice more (Psalm 42:11, Psalm 43:5), reinforcing the discipline of choosing trust over fear.

PSALM 77 FROM DESPAIR TO
REMEMBERING GOD'S FAITHFULNESS

Psalm 77 follows a similar pattern but gives even greater insight into how lament moves from anxiety to trust. The psalmist begins in deep distress "I cried out to God for help; I cried out to God to hear me. When I was in distress, I sought the Lord; at night

I stretched out untiring hands, and I would not be comforted" (Psalm 77:1–2).

This is raw, unfiltered pain. He prays, but there is no immediate relief. His mind spirals into doubt "Will the Lord reject forever? Will he never show his favor again? Has his unfailing love vanished forever? Has his promise failed for all time?" (Psalm 77:7–8). Here, the psalmist voices the questions anxiety often brings, "Has God forgotten me? Does he still care?" This is the honesty of biblical lament. It doesn't rush to tidy answers; it acknowledges the reality of suffering.

But then, in verse 10, everything shifts. The psalmist makes a choice "Then I thought, 'To this I will appeal, the years when the Most High stretched out his right hand. I will remember the deeds of the Lord; yes, I will remember your miracles of long ago' "(Psalm 77:10–11).

Instead of dwelling on uncertainty, he remembers. He recalls God's past faithfulness, his miracles, his acts of deliverance. He brings his mind back to truth, declaring "Your ways, God, are holy. What god is as great as our God? You are the God who performs miracles; you display your power among the peoples" (Psalm 77:13–14).

This is the power of lament; it doesn't end in despair but in worship. The psalmist's circumstances haven't changed, but his focus has. By remembering God's faithfulness, he finds renewed trust.

HOW LAMENT TRANSFORMS OUR OWN ANXIETY

Psalm 42 and Psalm 77 show us that lament isn't merely venting emotions; it's an intentional process that transforms our hearts from anxiety to trust. Lament gives voice to our anxiety, instead of suppressing fears, we bring them honestly before God, knowing he hears and cares (Psalm 42:3, Psalm 77:1–2). Lament confronts anxious thoughts with truth, the psalmists both speak directly to their souls, choosing to recall who God is instead of dwelling on fear (Psalm 42:5, Psalm 77:11–12). Lament leads to worship, as we remind ourselves of the biblical truth of God's faithfulness, anxiety loses its grip, and trust in God's sovereignty grows stronger (Psalm 77:13–14).

Biblical lament is one of the most powerful tools for overcoming anxiety because it doesn't ignore pain, it transforms it into deeper trust in God. As we learn to practice lament, we begin to experience the shift from anxiety to the peace that comes from resting in God's faithfulness.

Next, we'll explore how to practice lament, following the biblical steps of crying out, remembering, surrendering, and praising God even in the midst of anxiety.

PRACTICING LAMENT

Lament is a biblically grounded process that brings our anxieties and fears before God in a way that transforms them into trust. Through lament, we engage deeply and honestly with our emotions, allowing God's truth to reorient our hearts. The biblical practice of lament moves through four essential steps, Cry Out, Remember, Surrender, and Praise. These steps are evident throughout Scripture, and one of the most profound examples is found in Psalm 13, where David moves from deep despair to confident praise.

STEP I CRY OUT BRINGING YOUR HONEST PAIN TO GOD

The first step in biblical lament is to cry out to God honestly and openly. Too often, anxiety convinces us to suppress our fears or pretend they don't exist, but lament calls us to express our deepest concerns without shame. This isn't about accusing God or giving in to despair but about acknowledging the reality of our pain and bringing it directly before the one who cares.

David opens Psalm 13 with unfiltered anguish "How long, Lord? Will you forget me forever? How long will you hide your face from me? How long must I wrestle with my thoughts and day after day have sorrow in my heart? How long will my enemy triumph over me?" (Psalm 13:1–2).

David's cry is both desperate and bold. He doesn't hide his pain or minimize his struggle. Four times he cries, "How long?" a clear sign that he feels overwhelmed and abandoned. He is honest about his wrestling thoughts and the sorrow that grips his heart. Yet, despite his fear and frustration, he directs his cry to God, demonstrating his faith that God is the one who can hear and respond.

In this first step, it's essential to break the silence that anxiety creates. Crying out to God is an act of surrender, admitting that we cannot carry the burden on our own. It's also a declaration that we believe God is compassionate enough to hear our pain and strong enough to respond.

How to Practice This Step

1. Speak openly to God about what is troubling you.

2. Write out your lament in a journal, using David's honesty as a model.

3. Allow yourself to be vulnerable with God, admitting your fear, doubt, or sadness without filtering your emotions.

STEP 2 REMEMBER CALLING TO MIND GOD'S CHARACTER

After crying out, lament moves toward remembering who God is, it could be, God's faithfulness, his mercy, his unfailing love, etc. This step is crucial because anxiety distorts our perception of reality, making us forget how God has provided and sustained us in the past. Instead of allowing fear to cloud our minds, biblical lament intentionally recalls who God is and what he has done.

In Psalm 13, David makes a pivotal turn "But I trust in your unfailing love; my heart rejoices in your salvation" (Psalm 13:5).

Here, David shifts from despair to deliberate trust. He chooses to remember God's unfailing love and rejoice in his salvation, even though his situation hasn't changed. This act of remembering isn't about denying reality but about allowing truth to speak louder than fear.

When anxiety whispers that we are forgotten or abandoned, remembering God's faithfulness anchors us in the reality that he never leaves or forsakes us (Deuteronomy 31:8). Reflecting on past experiences where God has proven faithful helps restore confidence, reminding us that his character is unwavering despite our circumstances.

How to Practice This Step

1. Reflect on past moments when God has shown his faithfulness (or other attributes) in your life. Write them down as reminders.

2. Meditate on Scripture that highlights God's unchanging character and his care for his people (Psalm 103, Isaiah 41:10).

3. Speak truth to your own heart from God's word, reminding yourself of God's goodness and faithfulness, even when emotions try to tell a different story.

STEP 3 SURRENDER—RELEASING CONTROL AND TRUSTING GOD

Lament isn't complete without surrender. After crying out and remembering God's faithfulness, we must release our anxious grip on our circumstances. Anxiety feeds on our desire to control outcomes but surrender means relinquishing that need and trusting God to work in ways we cannot see.

David exemplifies this surrender as he concludes Psalm 13 "I will sing the Lord's praise, for he has been good to me" (Psalm 13:6). Even without resolution, David chooses to trust and sing

God's praise. His heart shifts from anxiety to resting, from controlling to submitting. Surrender means acknowledging that God is
sovereign, wise, and good, even when life feels chaotic. It's recognizing that our understanding is limited, but God's is infinite.

Surrender isn't passive resignation; it's an active decision to
place the burden on God rather than bearing it ourselves. This is
the heart of Philippians 4:6–7, where Paul calls believers to present
their requests to God with thanksgiving, allowing God's peace to
guard their hearts and minds.

How to Practice This Step

1. Pray specifically, naming the fears you are surrendering to
   God.
2. Write out a prayer of surrender, releasing control and asking
   God to take over.

STEP 4 PRAISE—DECLARING GOD'S WORTHINESS EVEN IN THE WAITING

Lament doesn't end with defeat but with praise. This isn't because
every problem is resolved, but because God is worthy of worship
regardless of our circumstances. Praising God after lament is an
act of faith, proclaiming that his goodness remains even when life
is uncertain.

David closes his lament in Psalm 13 by choosing to sing to
the Lord. This choice to worship isn't driven by a change in situation but by a steadfast belief that God is still worthy. Praise in
lament isn't about denying pain, but about exalting God above the
weight of anxiety.

By choosing to praise God in the midst of distress, we declare
that anxiety doesn't have the final say—God does. We affirm that
he is faithful, powerful, and ever-present, despite our fluctuating

emotions. This step solidifies the journey of lament, lifting our eyes from our worries to the one who is greater than them all.

How to Practice This Step

1. Play a hymn or worship song that reminds you of God's character and sovereignty.

2. Write a list of attributes of God that are true regardless of your situation.

3. Choose one Scripture to memorize that declares God's worthiness (Psalm 34:1, Psalm 145:3).

LAMENT VS. COMPLAINING, UNDERSTANDING THE DIFFERENCE

Distinguishing between lament and sinful complaining is essential. While both involve expressing hardship, they stem from vastly different heart postures, a distinction clearly illustrated in Scripture. Consider Numbers 11 and Psalm 10.

In Numbers 11, the Israelites grumble about God's provision, yearning for Egyptian food instead of appreciating the manna he provided. Their complaints, fueled by ingratitude and entitlement, aren't a humble appeal to God but a discontented murmur among themselves. This questioning of God's goodness provoked his anger.

Psalm 10 offers a contrasting example. David, in anguish, asks, "Why, O Lord, do you stand far away?" (Psalm 10:1). Unlike the Israelites, David directs his lament to God, not merely about him. His heart is rightly oriented, bringing pain and questions to the only One who can truly answer. The psalm concludes not in despair but with David reaffirming God's sovereignty and justice, even amidst unresolved pain.

The crucial difference lies in the heart's attitude. Complaining questions God's character, fueled by inward focus, dissatisfaction, and disbelief, assuming we deserve better. Lament, however, expresses sorrow and confusion while acknowledging God's sovereignty and goodness, directing pain toward him, not against him. From a biblical counseling perspective, lament opens the door for God to meet us in our pain and reorient our hearts toward his truth.

THE TRANSFORMATIVE POWER OF LAMENT

Practicing biblical lament through these four steps Cry Out, Remember, Surrender, Praise, creates a pathway from anxiety to trust. Lament doesn't ignore the reality of fear or pain, but it refuses to be dominated by them. Instead, lament teaches us to bring our burdens before God, ground our hearts in his faithfulness, relinquish control, and ultimately worship him despite uncertainty.

When we learn to lament biblically, we discover that anxiety loses its grip, and faith takes root. Lament isn't a one-time event but a continual practice, as long as life in a fallen world presents struggles. Yet through it all, God's invitation remains to cry out, to remember his goodness, to surrender control, and to lift our hearts in praise. In doing so, we find peace not because every situation is resolved, but because our trust has shifted from ourselves to the faithful hands of God.

CHAPTER SUMMARY

Lament is a sacred process that moves us from anxiety to trust by guiding our hearts through an intentional pattern rooted in Scripture Cry Out, Remember, Surrender, Praise. It's more than simply venting frustration; it's a biblical practice that draws us closer to God in our pain. Crying out allows us to honestly express our deepest struggles without fear of judgment, laying our burdens openly before the Lord. Remembering helps us ground our minds in God's past faithfulness, reminding us that he is steadfast and trustworthy despite our current fears. Surrendering shifts the weight of control from our shoulders to God's, acknowledging that his sovereignty is greater than our striving. Finally, praising God, even amidst unresolved circumstances, lifts our gaze from our anxiety to the God who holds all things together.

Through the practice of lamenting, we learn to navigate anxiety not by avoiding it but by confronting it with faith. Biblical lament doesn't end in despair but in worship, affirming that God remains worthy of praise regardless of our emotions or circumstances. As we incorporate this practice into our lives, anxiety loses its grip, and peace takes root—not because every struggle is resolved, but because we have anchored our trust in God's unchanging character.

HOMEWORK ASSIGNMENTS

Practicing Personal Lament

Choose one specific area of anxiety that feels heavy on your heart. Spend some quiet time in prayer or journaling, allowing yourself to be honest with God about your fears and anxieties. Start by crying out to God, expressing your thoughts and emotions without holding anything back. Then, take a moment to remember God's faithfulness in the past and how he has shown his goodness in your life. Surrender your anxiety to him, releasing control and trusting that he will work in his wisdom and timing. Finally, end by praising God for his unchanging character and faithfulness, even if the situation hasn't changed. Reflect on how your perspective shifts through this process, and write down any changes in your thoughts or feelings.

Memorize and Meditate on a Psalm of Lament

Select a psalm of lament from the Bible, such as Psalm 13 or Psalm 142. Spend a few minutes each day reading and reflecting on a portion of the psalm, letting its words sink into your heart. As you memorize parts of it, notice how the psalmist balances honesty and faith. Use the psalm as a personal prayer, letting its words guide your own expressions of lament before God. At the end of the week, look back and consider how meditating on this psalm has shaped your understanding of lament and affected your experience with anxiety.

Reflective Questions

1. What does your current prayer life reveal about your willingness to bring God your deepest worries?

2. When you lament, are you in your heart open to replacing sorrow with praise?

4

Anxiety as a Reflection
of Our View of God

OUR BELIEFS ABOUT GOD profoundly shape every aspect of our lives, influencing our thoughts, emotions, choices, and especially our anxieties. Anxiety is a spiritual indicator, revealing what we truly believe about God. When anxiety grips us, it often signals that we've lost sight of God's true character. Instead of resting in his faithfulness, sovereignty, and love, we become consumed by fear and doubt, subtly indicating a distorted view of God.

At the root of nearly every anxious thought lies a misconception about God's nature. These distortions develop gradually through difficult experiences, unmet expectations, disappointments, and the influence of a fallen world. Scripture continually invites us to correct these distortions by returning to the truth of who God has revealed himself to be in the Bible. Correcting misconceptions about who God is can only be impacted by a concerted effort to read and study the Bible.

COMMON DISTORTED VIEWS OF GOD

To recognize how anxiety reflects our distorted views of God, we must first identify common misconceptions. Here are four frequent distortions.

God as distant or uncaring. One common distortion views God as distant, uninvolved, or indifferent to our struggles. We might intellectually acknowledge his existence but practically believe he's disconnected from our daily lives. This perception causes anxiety, leaving us feeling alone and responsible for navigating life's uncertainties without God's help.

When we believe God is distant, our anxiety intensifies. We interpret hardships or unanswered prayers as evidence of his absence or lack of care. Yet Scripture refutes this distorted view. God assures us of his close and compassionate presence "The Lord is close to the brokenhearted and saves those who are crushed in spirit" (Psalm 34:18). "Cast all your anxiety on him because he cares for you" (1 Peter 5:7).

If we truly believe these promises, anxiety loses its power because we trust we are never abandoned, even when life feels overwhelming. This trust is a cornerstone of biblical peace.

God as critical or harsh. Another distorted view sees God primarily as judgmental, harsh, or demanding. When we envision God as an angry judge, we become anxious, constantly fearing punishment or rejection. This fosters a cycle of anxiety driven by performance and perfectionism, making us believe our acceptance depends solely on our ability to measure up.

Such a view creates an exhausting spiritual life defined by fear rather than faith. But Scripture paints a different picture "The Lord is compassionate and gracious, slow to anger, abounding in love. . .he does not treat us as our sins deserve or repay us according to our iniquities" (Psalm 103:8, 10).

When we embrace God's true nature, loving, gracious, and forgiving, our anxiety diminishes, replaced by confident assurance in his mercy. This assurance is a gift of grace, freely offered through faith.

God as limited or powerless. Sometimes our anxiety stems from a distorted view that sees God as limited or incapable of handling our circumstances. When life feels chaotic, we might unconsciously question God's ability to manage our problems. Anxiety thrives when we perceive our problems as bigger than God.

However, the Bible asserts God's limitless strength and sovereignty "Surely the arm of the Lord is not too short to save, nor his ear too dull to hear" (Isaiah 59:1). "I am the Lord, the God of all mankind. Is anything too hard for me?" (Jeremiah 32:27).

Believing in God's infinite power confronts anxiety, reassuring us that nothing we face can overwhelm or surprise him. Our fears lose their potency when we see God accurately powerful enough to sustain us in every circumstance. Biblical hope is rooted in this understanding of God's omnipotence.

God as unreliable or unfaithful. Perhaps most destructive to our peace is the distortion that portrays God as unreliable, unpredictable, or unfaithful. We may have experienced betrayal or disappointment in relationships and unintentionally transferred those experiences onto God. If we doubt God's trustworthiness, anxiety naturally follows because we become uncertain whether he will keep his promises.

Yet the biblical narrative emphasizes God's unwavering faithfulness "Know therefore that the Lord your God is God; he is the faithful God, keeping his covenant of love to a thousand generations. . ." (Deuteronomy 7:9). "If we are faithless, he remains faithful, for he cannot disown himself" (2 Timothy 2:13).

When we firmly anchor our hearts in the reliability of God's promises, anxiety begins to lose its foundation. We no longer wonder if God will abandon us because we know that his faithfulness is absolute and eternal. This assurance provides a stable foundation for our lives.

HOW CORRECTING OUR VIEW OF
GOD CHANGES OUR ANXIETY

Anxiety exposes gaps between what we profess about God and what we truly believe. Each anxious thought offers an opportunity to re-examine our beliefs and align them with biblical truth. When we understand who God genuinely is, compassionate, merciful, powerful, faithful, our anxiety diminishes, replaced by a trust rooted in his unchanging character. This aligns with biblical counseling, which emphasizes the transformative power of truth.

Imagine the profound change that occurs when we truly see God as he is. If we believe God is compassionate and caring, we find comfort knowing we're never alone in our suffering. Understanding God's mercy and grace frees us from the exhausting pressure of tying our worth to performance. Recognizing God's sovereignty brings peace, assuring us that no situation is beyond his control or redemption. Trusting in God's faithfulness allows us to depend on him, even when circumstances feel uncertain.

This renewed vision of God transforms us because anxiety often stems from deep questions about his character "Is he good? Can he be trusted? Will he truly care for me?" As we clearly see God as Scripture reveals him, anxiety loses its grip. In its place grows biblical hope—a confident expectation rooted in God's unchanging character.

REFLECTING ON OUR VIEW OF GOD

To address our anxieties, we must ask ourselves honestly "What do my anxieties reveal about what I truly believe about God?" Anxiety can become a tool for spiritual growth, revealing areas where our theology needs to deepen or corrected to align with biblical teaching. Rather than simply trying to control anxious feelings, we address anxiety by confronting and correcting distorted beliefs about God. This self-examination is crucial for spiritual maturity.

Moving forward, we will explore God's true character in greater depth, especially his sovereignty and absolute faithfulness, and how embracing these truths can shift our thinking from anxiety-filled "what if?" scenarios toward a faith-filled "even if" confidence. This shift empowers us to face life's uncertainties not with fear, but with steadfast hope anchored securely in who God is. This is the pathway to lasting peace and freedom from anxiety.

Ultimately, the battle against anxiety is won not by suppressing our fears but by seeing God rightly. As we allow Scripture to reshape our view of God, anxiety loses its grip, replaced by a deep and abiding trust in the one who knows us fully, loves us perfectly, and holds all things securely in his sovereign hands. This trust is the fruit of a transformed heart and mind, grounded in the truth of God's Word.

GOD'S SOVEREIGNTY AND CHARACTER (ISAIAH 46:9–10)

Anxiety often thrives when we feel life is chaotic or out of control. This stems from uncertainty about who is truly in charge. Scripture answers this God is sovereign, and his character is unchangingly good. Understanding and embracing these truths is crucial for biblically overcoming anxiety.

God's sovereignty means he holds absolute control over every circumstance. Nothing is random or outside his authority. Isaiah 46:9–10 expresses this "Remember the former things, those of long ago; I am God, and there is no other; I am God, and there is none like me. I make known the end from the beginning, from ancient times, what is still to come. I say, my purpose will stand, and I will do all that I please."

In this declaration, God emphasizes uniqueness and supremacy "I am God, and there is no other." God alone has ultimate authority, unequaled by anyone or anything. He is not competing with other powers or limited by outside forces. He alone reigns supreme.

Control over all history and time, "I make known the end from the beginning." Nothing escapes his view or happens without his permission. God isn't surprised by events. He knows every outcome, directing history toward his purpose.

These truths are comforting when anxiety tempts us to believe life is spinning out of control. If God is truly sovereign, anxiety loses its power. We can rest knowing our lives are held in the hands of a God whose control is perfect and whose purposes are always for our good (Romans 8:28).

GOD'S SOVEREIGNTY AND GOODNESS

Sovereignty alone doesn't fully comfort anxious hearts. Power without goodness could be terrifying. Thankfully, the Bible links God's sovereignty with his impeccable character. The God who controls all things is also perfectly good, loving, wise, and faithful. Sovereignty and goodness go hand in hand

God's sovereign rule is always rooted in his love. He doesn't orchestrate events arbitrarily or carelessly; instead, his governance is purposeful, intentional, and compassionate. Psalm 145:17 assures us, "The Lord is righteous in all his ways and faithful in all he does." Even when we face difficult times, we can trust that God's hand is guided by unwavering love (Psalm 136:1). This love is the bedrock of his sovereignty, a comforting truth in uncertain times.

Furthermore, God's sovereignty is characterized by infinite wisdom. He fully understands what is best for us, even when our understanding is limited. Isaiah 55:8–9 reminds us, "For my thoughts are not your thoughts, neither are your ways my ways," declares the Lord. "As the heavens are higher than the earth, so are my ways higher than your ways and my thoughts than your thoughts." When we struggle to understand why things happen, we can find peace in his superior wisdom. Knowing that he sees the bigger picture can bring solace and hope.

God's sovereignty guarantees his faithfulness. Because he reigns with absolute authority, every promise he makes is reliable. Numbers 23:19 declares, "God is not human, that he should lie. . .Does he speak and then not act? Does he promise and not fulfill?" When anxiety tempts us to doubt whether God will fulfill his promises, his unwavering faithfulness becomes our anchor, grounding us in hope and confidence. This faithfulness, born of his sovereign power and love, is a constant source of strength.

APPLYING GOD'S SOVEREIGNTY

Anxiety often stems from distorted views of God. To combat this, we must intentionally replace these distortions with biblical truth. Understanding God's sovereignty and character transforms how we respond to anxiety.

When life feels overwhelming, remember that God is in control. Anxiety diminishes as we trust that nothing is beyond his sovereign rule. Even the circumstances that trigger our anxiety are held securely in his hands, not subject to chance.

Furthermore, God is inherently good and loving. Recognizing that the one who governs all things does so with perfect love and compassion weakens anxiety's grip. Even when we don't understand, we can trust his heart, knowing he directs everything for our ultimate good and his glory.

God is infinitely wise and perfectly faithful. Anxiety tempts us to doubt God's plans or his promises. In those moments, cling to the truth of his unwavering wisdom and faithfulness. Every difficulty becomes an opportunity to experience his trustworthiness more deeply and to depend on his wisdom.

REFLECTING ON GOD'S SOVEREIGNTY

To truly combat anxiety, we must let the truth of God's sovereignty move beyond intellectual agreement and take root deeply within our hearts. Isaiah 46:9–10 isn't simply theological knowledge; it's a deeply personal promise from a God who genuinely cares for us. Because he holds absolute control, we no longer need to bear the exhausting burden of managing every detail of our lives. Instead, we can humbly surrender our worries into his capable hands.

Because God is sovereign, we don't have to fear uncertainty. He walks ahead of us into every unknown, preparing the path, providing what we need before we even ask. Our hearts can find rest and calm confidence in the assurance that he is already there, meeting us in every tomorrow. Even the most challenging situations we face are never random or meaningless, they are lovingly woven into God's redemptive purposes for our good and his glory.

As we anchor our trust in this truth, that the God who deeply loves us also faithfully governs every aspect of our lives, anxiety's grip naturally loosens. Moving forward, we'll explore how embracing God's sovereignty transforms anxious "what if?" worries into courageous "even if" faith, deeply grounded in the unwavering promise that no matter what happens, God's loving and sovereign character will never fail us.

FROM "WHAT IF?" WORRY TO "EVEN IF" FAITH

Anxiety often starts with the question, "What if?" This question can magnify our worries, tempting us to imagine the worst and subtly asking, "Will God still be good, faithful, and trustworthy if the worst happens?" "What if?" thinking can lead us to dwell on uncertain futures, inflating fears and undermining our confidence in God's power and goodness.

But scripture invites us to shift from anxious speculation to confident trust. Instead of letting fear dominate, we can embrace "Even if" faith—grounded not in desired outcomes, but in God's unchanging character.

THE TRAP OF "WHAT IF?" THINKING

When we get stuck in "What if?" thinking, our minds can feel overwhelmed with fearful possibilities—losing a job, facing illness, enduring broken relationships, or unanswered prayers. This breeds anxiety by focusing on uncertainties and subtly questioning God's faithfulness, stealing our peace.

God doesn't ask us to deny life's challenges but to trust him in the midst of them. Anchoring our hearts in his character frees us from anxious speculation. Faith rooted in God's unchanging nature releases us from fear's grip and brings peace even when circumstances feel unpredictable.

"EVEN IF" FAITH A BIBLICAL RESPONSE

Biblical faith isn't blind optimism but grounded confidence in God's unwavering character. "Even if" faith acknowledges uncertainties while affirming that God remains good, sovereign, and present. We see this vividly in Daniel 3, where Shadrach, Meshach, and Abednego stand before the fiery furnace and declare "If we are thrown into the blazing furnace, the God we serve is able to deliver us from it . . . But even if he does not, we want you to know, Your Majesty, that we will not serve your gods or worship the image of gold you have set up" (Daniel 3:17–18).

Their faith wasn't dependent on the outcome but rooted in unwavering trust in God. That's the essence of "Even if" faith, confidence anchored not in circumstances but in the nature of God himself.

IDENTIFYING AND CHALLENGING "WHAT IF?" THOUGHTS

Recognize when anxious thoughts arise and name the "What if?" questions that fuel them. Instead of spiraling into fear, intentionally challenge them with truth.

- "What if I lose my job?" becomes "Even if I lose my job, God has promised to provide for my needs" (Philippians 4 19).

- "What if my loved one becomes ill?" becomes "Even if sickness comes, God will never leave us" (Hebrews 13 5).

- "What if things don't go as planned?" becomes "Even if my plans fail, God works all things for my good and his glory" (Romans 8 28).

ANCHORING YOUR HEART IN GOD'S PROMISES

Saturate your thoughts with scripture that affirms God's character.

- God's Goodness "Taste and see that the lord is good blessed is the one who takes refuge in him" (Psalm 34 8).

- God's Faithfulness "Because of the lord's great love we are not consumed, for his compassions never fail. They are new every morning great is your faithfulness" (Lamentations 3 22–23).

- God's Presence "When you pass through the waters, I will be with you" (Isaiah 43 2).

EMBRACING SURRENDER AND DEPENDENCE

Anxiety often exposes our desire to control outcomes, but surrender means trusting that God's plans are better than ours—even when they differ from what we hoped. Paul's counsel in Philippians 4 6–7 reflects "Even if" faith—bringing every concern to God with thanksgiving, while trusting him to guard our hearts with his peace.

REHEARSE "EVEN IF" TRUTHS DAILY

Combat "What if?" thoughts by daily rehearsing "Even if" declarations.

- "Even if today brings hardship, God will sustain me."

- "Even if my prayers aren't answered as I hope, God's ways are better than mine."

- "Even if disappointment comes, God's love will never fail."

The difference between "What if?" and "Even if?" lies in how we view God. Anxiety questions his goodness, but faith proclaims that God is enough—even if fears become reality. This shift transforms anxiety from a burden to an opportunity to deepen trust, finding peace not in the absence of trouble but in the presence of our faithful God.

CHAPTER SUMMARY

This chapter explores how anxiety often reveals distorted beliefs about God's character, exposing the gap between what we profess and what our hearts truly believe. Misconceptions, seeing God as distant, harsh, powerless, or unreliable, fuel anxious thoughts, leaving us feeling overwhelmed. Scripture calls us to correct these views by embracing God as he truly is sovereign, faithful, loving, and wise.

We examined how God's sovereignty, declared in Isaiah 46:9–10, reassures us that nothing is beyond his control. Understanding God as both sovereign and good helps us face anxiety with trust, not fear. We also discussed shifting from "what if?" thinking to "even if" faith, grounding our trust in God's unchanging character rather than hypothetical fears.

"Even if" faith, exemplified by Shadrach, Meshach, and Abednego in Daniel 3, demonstrates trusting God regardless of the outcome. This faith is rooted in the unwavering confidence that God's character remains steadfast, no matter what. Moving from "what if?" to "even if" helps us live with peace, knowing God's sovereignty and goodness are greater than any challenge.

HOMEWORK ASSIGNMENTS

Practicing Faith Statements

When anxiety confronts you with a "What if?" question, practice responding with a biblical truth or faith statement. Begin by writing down some of the common "What if?" thoughts that trouble you, like "What if I lose my job?" or "What if this relationship fails?" Next to each thought, write a truth rooted in Scripture, such as "Even if I lose my job, God will still provide for me" (Philippians 4:19). This exercise will help you intentionally shift your perspective from fear to faith, reminding your heart of God's promises in moments of uncertainty.

Reflective Questions

1. How does your view of God shape your response to anxiety? What might need to change in your perception of his character?

2. In what ways can shifting from "What if?" thinking to "Even if" faith help you grow spiritually?

Examining Distorted Views of God

Choose one area of anxiety that recurs in your life and take some time to honestly examine what it might reveal about your view of God. Ask yourself whether your anxiety stems from seeing God as distant, harsh, powerless, or unreliable. Once you identify the distortion, find a Scripture that directly counters it with truth. For example, if you struggle with feeling that God is distant, reflect on Psalm 34:18, which says, "The Lord is close to the brokenhearted and saves those who are crushed in spirit."

Spend time in prayer, confessing any distorted views of God that have shaped your thinking, and ask him to replace them with the truth of who he really is. As you continue this exercise with different anxieties that arise, you will gradually train your heart to see God rightly, strengthening your faith and deepening your trust in his unwavering character.

5

The Power of Prayer in Overcoming Anxiety

PRAYER IS MORE THAN a spiritual discipline; it's an act of surrender, acknowledging our dependence on God. Anxiety often thrives when we try to control what we can't. Prayer redirects us to humble dependence, reminding us that we are needy, reliant, and safe in the care of a sovereign and compassionate Father.

Philippians 4:6–7 beautifully illustrates prayer as surrender "Do not be anxious about anything, but in every situation, by prayer and petition, with thanksgiving, present your requests to God. And the peace of God, which transcends all understanding, will guard your hearts and your minds in Christ Jesus." Paul's words offer practical guidance and spiritual wisdom. We are to surrender every anxious thought and circumstance to God in prayer. Prayer isn't just a coping mechanism; it's our primary response to anxiety.

The Greek word for "present" means "to lay before" or "to entrust." Prayer isn't just asking God to fix a problem; it's intentionally releasing our burdens into his capable hands. This acknowledges his sovereignty, letting go of worry and resting in his provision.

Similarly, 1 Peter 5:7 emphasizes prayer as active surrender "Cast all your anxiety on him because he cares for you." Peter emphasizes the importance of casting our anxieties onto God, reminding us that the reason we can confidently do so is because God genuinely and deeply cares for us. Instead of silently nursing anxiety, we intentionally transfer its weight to God, trusting him fully.

The heart of prayer as surrender is the conviction that we can't bear anxiety alone, but God is sufficient. Anxiety diminishes as we recognize that our loving Father never intended us to face life's uncertainties alone. He invites us to surrender our worries, fears, and anxieties to him, confident in his love and power.

JESUS' MODEL OF PRAYER IN SUFFERING (MATTHEW 26:39)

For a deeper understanding of prayer as surrender, we look to Jesus. His life exemplifies praying through anxiety and suffering. The night before his crucifixion, in the Garden of Gethsemane, he prayed, knowing the suffering ahead. His prayer in Matthew 26:39 is a model for approaching anxiety "Going a little farther, he fell with his face to the ground and prayed, 'My Father, if it is possible, may this cup be taken from me. Yet not as I will, but as you will.'"

JESUS MODELS THREE ASPECTS OF PRAYERFUL SURRENDER

Jesus exemplifies authentic honesty by openly expressing his distress, free from reservation or stoicism. His heartfelt prayer in the garden, asking the Father to remove his suffering, reassures us that God is neither surprised nor disappointed by our emotions. Instead, he lovingly invites us to bring our fears and anxieties to him, knowing he fully understands.

But Jesus doesn't stop at honesty; he intentionally surrenders to God's will, praying, "Yet not as I will, but as you will." This surrender is central to biblical prayer—acknowledging our desires while entrusting them to God's greater wisdom. Jesus submitted his anguish to his Father, modeling how to trust God's purposes above our own, even in great difficulty.

At the heart of Jesus' prayer is a deep trust in God's goodness and sovereignty. Even facing unimaginable suffering, Jesus confidently rested in the Father's perfect plan and character. This transforms mere resignation into faithful surrender, placing our anxieties and uncertainties into the care of our loving, trustworthy Father.

Jesus' example speaks powerfully to our anxieties. By honestly pouring out our fears before God and surrendering our situations to his control, we imitate Christ. We align our hearts with God's will and experience the peace that follows.

FROM ANXIETY TO PEACE, THE PATH OF SURRENDER

The power of biblical prayer lies in transferring our anxieties from our control to God's sovereignty. Philippians 4:6–7 and 1 Peter 5:7 highlight that prayer is actively relinquishing control, casting anxieties onto the God who cares for us.

As Jesus modeled, prayerful surrender acknowledges suffering and anxiety, yet rests in God's care and purpose. When we pray this way, anxiety loses its power because it rests in God's strength, love, and wisdom.

The result is a peace "which transcends all understanding," guarding our hearts and minds in Christ Jesus. Prayer becomes laying our anxieties at the feet of our sovereign, compassionate God. As we follow Christ's example, we rest in God's character, not outcomes. This surrender, modeled by Jesus, is the pathway from anxiety to peace.

FINDING PEACE AT NIGHT

Nighttime anxiety can feel overwhelming. As the day's distractions fade, worries and fears often intensify, invading our hearts and minds. During these vulnerable hours, anxiety can amplify our fears, leading to restless nights and racing thoughts. Yet, Scripture assures us that even in the darkest nights, God's presence, comfort, and peace remain steadfast and accessible through prayer and meditation on his Word.

King David, whose life was marked by trials, intimately understood nighttime anxiety. In Psalm 4:8, he confidently declares "In peace I will lie down and sleep, for you alone, Lord, make me dwell in safety."

David's peace wasn't found in perfect circumstances, but in his trust in the Lord's presence and protection. He intentionally chose to rest, trusting that God alone secured his safety. This intentional trust is key to overcoming nighttime anxiety. Anxiety often tries to convince us that we are alone, but Scripture repeatedly affirms that God is always near, guarding us as we rest.

SCRIPTURE AS AN ANCHOR IN THE NIGHT

Scripture provides a powerful weapon against anxiety, especially when our minds are most vulnerable. By meditating on God's promises and character, we anchor our hearts in truths stronger than any fear. Psalm 119:148 illustrates this "My eyes stay open through the watches of the night, that I may meditate on your promises."

Instead of surrendering to anxious thoughts, the psalmist intentionally redirects his mind toward God's promises and faithfulness. Similarly, Psalm 63:6–8 describes this intentional nighttime meditation "On my bed I remember you; I think of you through the watches of the night. Because you are my help, I sing in the shadow of your wings. I cling to you; your right hand upholds me."

These verses show a deliberate choice to replace anxious thoughts with a focus on God's faithfulness and protection. The psalmist actively recalls God's goodness, declares God's help, and clings to God's presence.

When nighttime anxiety threatens our peace, we must practice this same intentional meditation. By reflecting on specific

Scriptures that reveal God's character, promises, and faithfulness, we anchor our minds to truths stronger than any anxious thought.

ENTRUSTING ANXIETIES TO GOD

Prayer complements Scripture meditation by providing a direct channel to surrender our anxieties to God. Nighttime prayer is a lifeline of communication, comfort, and surrender.

David models this in Psalm 56:3-4 "When I am afraid, I put my trust in you. In God, whose word I praise, in God I trust and am not afraid."

David acknowledges his fear yet chooses trust through prayer. His prayers actively engage his heart with God, moving him from fear toward trust. When we approach nighttime anxiety with prayer, we acknowledge our fears openly before God, casting our burdens onto God who cares for us (1 Peter 5:7).

When nighttime anxiety arises, prayer offers a powerful path to comfort and peace. Begin by honestly sharing your anxieties with God, naming each fear openly and clearly. He welcomes sincere conversation and invites you to share your burdens without hesitation. As you pray, intentionally declare God's promises, anchoring your prayers in specific biblical truths. For example, if loneliness troubles you, gently remind yourself of the assurance in Hebrews 13:5 "I will never leave you nor forsake you." Consciously surrender control, releasing each worry into God's capable hands, trusting fully in his wisdom and timing. Express this surrender by praying, "Lord, I entrust this anxiety to you, confident that your ways are best." Furthermore, praying Scripture can significantly ease anxious thoughts. Choose verses that directly address your fears, praying through them slowly and thoughtfully, allowing the truth of God's Word to renew your mind and align your heart with his peace.

PRACTICAL STEPS FOR NIGHTTIME PEACE

To ease nighttime anxiety, prepare your mind with Scripture before bed. Reading or quietly reciting comforting passages that speak to God's care and peace can be very helpful. Consider verses like Psalm 23, Psalm 91, Philippians 4:6–7, and Isaiah 26:3–4. Writing these verses down and keeping them nearby allows you to meditate on these truths as you fall asleep.

Establishing a consistent nighttime prayer routine can also ease anxiety. Each evening, dedicate time to honestly and regularly present your worries to God, entrusting your heart and burdens to the One who never sleeps, as Psalm 121:4 reminds us.

Practicing God-centered breathing and reflection can also bring peace. As you lie down, intentionally slow your breathing, pairing each breath with simple prayers or Scripture phrases. For example, as you inhale, silently pray, "Lord, you are with me," and as you exhale, affirm, "I trust you completely." This rhythm calms your body and spirit, gently reminding you of God's faithful presence.

Finally, keeping a Scripture and prayer journal by your bedside provides a practical way to respond when anxiety disrupts your sleep. Jotting down Scriptures, personal prayers, and reminders of God's past faithfulness allows you to visibly release your anxieties into his care. This journaling practice lessens anxiety's grip and creates a meaningful record of God's ongoing care and reassurance in your life

RESTING SECURE IN GOD'S PEACE

Ultimately, overcoming nighttime anxiety involves turning our thoughts toward God and surrendering our fears through Scripture and prayer. When we practice this discipline, God's promise of peace becomes tangible. Nighttime anxiety no longer has the final word, instead, God's presence becomes our resting place.

As we meditate on his promises, surrender our anxieties in prayer, and trust in his care, we experience the truth of Isaiah 26:3

"You will keep in perfect peace those whose minds are steadfast, because they trust in you."

In the quiet of night, when anxiety seeks to overwhelm us, we can lean into God's presence, secure in the knowledge that his faithfulness is greater than our fears, and his peace stronger than our anxieties.

CHAPTER SUMMARY

This chapter explores how prayer, as an act of surrender, directly addresses anxiety. Anxiety often stems from trying to control the uncontrollable. Prayer redirects our focus, fostering dependence on God's sovereign care. Drawing from Philippians 4:6–7 and 1 Peter 5:7, we learn that prayer involves actively entrusting our anxieties to a compassionate and sovereign God, releasing control and experiencing profound peace.

We also examined Jesus' prayerful surrender in Gethsemane (Matthew 26:39) as a model. Even in extreme distress, Jesus demonstrated honesty, surrender, and deep trust in God's goodness. Furthermore, we discussed nighttime anxiety, highlighting the power of Scripture and prayer to find rest in God's presence during vulnerable moments.

By surrendering our anxieties in prayer and grounding our minds in God's promises, we can experience a peace that surpasses understanding—a peace rooted in God's unchanging character.

HOMEWORK ASSIGNMENTS

Developing a Daily Surrender Routine

Take some time to reflect on specific areas of your life where you find it difficult to surrender control to God. Think honestly and prayerfully about where anxiety holds its strongest grip. Once you have identified these areas, write down three of them in your journal, along with a verse that speaks of God's sovereignty and care.

Some examples might include Isaiah 41:10, *"So do not fear, for I am with you; do not be dismayed, for I am your God."*

Commit to keeping a journal where you can record how your mindset shifts over time and how God responds to your prayers. Make it a practice to regularly revisit your journal to see how surrendering to God has impacted your perspective and peace. Notice how your heart gradually learns to rest in his faithfulness as you entrust your worries to him.

Creating a Nighttime Routine for Peace

Establish a calming bedtime routine that intentionally centers your thoughts on God's faithfulness. Choose three to five verses that anchor your heart in his care and read them slowly before going to sleep. As you meditate on these truths, spend a few quiet moments in prayer, surrendering your fears and anxieties to God. Ask him to cover you with his peace, grant restful sleep, and keep watch over your heart through the night.

After your prayer, take a moment to write down one or two thoughts from your reflection or any insight you gained from the Scripture. Let this simple practice become a peaceful habit that helps you unwind and realign your heart with God's presence. This routine will become a signal to your mind and spirit that God is your protector and provider, allowing you to rest securely in his love.

Reflective Questions

1. What does your current prayer life reveal about your willingness to surrender control to God?

2. How can the example of Jesus praying in Gethsemane (Matthew 26:36–46) influence the way you handle your most anxious moments?

6

Finding Peace in Christ

IN THE PREVIOUS CHAPTER, we explored how prayer can help us overcome anxiety, finding peace not in controlling our circumstances, but in surrendering to God's loving care. Prayer aligns our hearts with his sovereign purposes, freeing us from the burdens of anxiety.

Yet, prayer points us to an even deeper source of peace, Jesus Christ. Lasting peace depends not on how we pray, but on whom we pray to. We now focus on Jesus, recognizing that our peace is founded on his finished work on the cross.

Anxiety often reveals uncertainty about our standing with God, whispering doubts about his acceptance, goodness, and love. It tempts us to question his care or to believe we must earn his favor. In these moments, we need a renewed understanding of the gospel, Christ's sacrifice is complete and sufficient.

On the cross, Jesus declared, "It is finished" (John 19:30). This powerful statement is the cornerstone of peace for every believer. But what did Jesus mean, and how does this truth transform anxiety into lasting peace?

UNDERSTANDING "IT IS FINISHED"

The phrase "It is finished" (John 19:30) signifies completion, fulfillment, and full satisfaction. On the cross, Jesus completed everything necessary for our salvation. He fully paid the penalty for our sin, absorbing the judgment we deserved, reconciling us to God once and for all. His death accomplished what no human effort could, perfect and complete peace with God.

Paul beautifully describes this in Romans 5:1 "Therefore, since we have been justified through faith, we have peace with God through our Lord Jesus Christ." This verse reveals a profound truth, peace with God is not something we achieve, but something Christ has already accomplished. Through his finished work, we no longer live under the weight of uncertainty, wondering if God accepts or loves us. Instead, we rest securely in Christ's perfect righteousness, fully accepted and eternally loved.

This truth confronts our anxieties, which often stem from striving and uncertainty. We wonder if we've done enough to merit God's favor. The gospel assures us that his love and acceptance are based entirely on Christ's completed work, not our performance. Our peace with God is secured by his sacrifice, not our strength.

TRANSFORMING ANXIETY INTO PEACE THROUGH CHRIST'S FINISHED WORK

When we anchor our hearts in Christ's finished work, anxiety loses its power. Here's why.

Complete forgiveness and acceptance. Anxiety thrives on guilt, shame, and uncertainty about our standing with God. Christ's death assures us that our sins—past, present, and future—are fully forgiven. Colossians 2:13–14 says "He forgave us all our sins, having canceled the charge of our legal indebtedness . . . nailing it to the cross." Our peace is unshakeable because it rests on Christ's permanent work, not our efforts.

Security in God's unchanging love. Anxiety convinces us we must earn God's approval, leading to spiritual and emotional exhaustion. Christ's finished work declares that God's love is steadfast and unconditional. Romans 8:38–39 promises that nothing can separate us from God's love in Christ. This truth transforms anxious striving into restful assurance.

Freedom from performance-based anxiety. The gospel frees us from striving for perfection. Instead of trying to earn God's favor, we rest in Christ's perfection on our behalf. Hebrews 10:14 says "For by one sacrifice he has made perfect forever those who are being made holy." When we grasp that our perfection and acceptance before God are fully provided by Christ, anxiety loses its power to accuse us.

LIVING IN LIGHT OF CHRIST'S FINISHED WORK

To experience this peace daily, we must continually return to the gospel and anchor our identity in Christ's completed sacrifice. Replace anxious thoughts with gospel truths, reminding ourselves of the certainty of our salvation and the security we have in Jesus.

This involves repeatedly preaching the gospel to ourselves. When anxiety whispers doubts or condemnation, respond confidently "My acceptance with God is fully secured in Christ's finished work." "I am loved because of Christ, not my performance." "God's love and peace are mine because of Christ, not my strength or perfection."

As we rehearse these truths daily, the peace of Christ becomes a tangible reality. Our anxiety gives way to trust because our peace is founded on the finished, unchanging, and perfect work of Christ.

THE ROLE OF THE HOLY SPIRIT

Experiencing peace in Christ is also the transforming work of the Holy Spirit in our hearts. In the next section, we will explore how the Holy Spirit applies these gospel truths to our lives, empowering us to overcome anxiety with the supernatural peace only God can provide.

Understanding and resting in Christ's finished work is foundational to experiencing peace, but God doesn't leave us to internalize and apply these truths alone. He graciously provides the Holy Spirit, who plays an essential role in helping us overcome anxiety and walk confidently in the peace Christ secured.

The Holy Spirit isn't merely an abstract force; he is God's personal presence dwelling within every believer. Jesus promised this gift, knowing we would need constant comfort, guidance, and strength as we navigate life's anxieties and challenges. In John 14:26–27, Jesus beautifully describes the Spirit's ministry "But the Advocate, the Holy Spirit, whom the Father will send in my name, will teach you all things and will remind you of everything I have said to you. Peace I leave with you; my peace I give you." Here, Jesus explicitly connects the Holy Spirit's presence with experiencing his peace. The Spirit is described as an advocate—one who comes alongside us to comfort, encourage, and reassure. Anxiety often isolates us, magnifying fears and making us feel alone. However, the Spirit breaks this isolation by continually reminding us of Christ's words and presence, reassuring us that we are never abandoned or forgotten.

HOW THE HOLY SPIRIT HELPS
US OVERCOME ANXIETY

To understand how the Spirit practically helps us battle anxiety, consider these key roles.

The Holy Spirit reminds us of truth. Anxiety thrives on uncertainty and confusion. It whispers doubts and distorts reality, leading us away from truth into fear. The Holy Spirit counters anxiety's voice by actively reminding us of the truths of Scripture, particularly truths about who God is and who we are in Christ. Jesus assured his disciples that the Spirit would "teach you all things and remind you of everything I have said" (John 14:26). When anxiety threatens to overwhelm us, the Spirit gently and persistently reminds our hearts of God's faithfulness, Christ's sufficiency, and the unchanging promises of God's Word.

This ongoing ministry of reminding is vital, especially when anxiety distorts our perspective. By constantly directing us back to Scripture, the Spirit grounds our hearts in the stability of God's promises, disarming anxiety's power to deceive us.

The Holy Spirit comforts and strengthens us. The Holy Spirit is described as our Advocate, one who draws near to encourage, strengthen, and reassure. Romans 8:26 vividly portrays this comforting ministry "In the same way, the Spirit helps us in our weakness. We do not know what we ought to pray for, but the Spirit himself intercedes for us through wordless groans." When anxiety leaves us speechless or overwhelmed, the Spirit steps in, praying with and for us, expressing our deepest needs and pains to the Father. His comforting presence reassures us that we are deeply known, understood, and cared for by God, even when we lack words to express our anxieties clearly.

The Holy Spirit empowers us to trust God. Anxiety often tempts us to rely on our own limited strength or to give in to despair when life seems out of control. The Holy Spirit, however, empowers us to place our trust fully in God. Galatians 5:22 describes peace as a direct fruit of the Holy Spirit's presence within us. This peace is supernatural, not produced by human effort but cultivated by the Spirit's active presence.

When anxiety rises, the Spirit strengthens us from within, enabling us to choose trust rather than fear. He actively works within our hearts, cultivating trust in God's character, promises, and sovereignty, empowering us to surrender anxiety and embrace God's peace.

COOPERATING WITH THE HOLY SPIRIT

Experiencing the Holy Spirit's powerful work in overcoming anxiety involves intentionally cooperating with his ministry through daily dependence, saturating our minds with Scripture, and responsive obedience. Each day, we must consciously invite the Holy Spirit to guide, comfort, and remind us of God's truth, actively depending on his strength rather than our own. Regularly reading, meditating on, and memorizing Scripture creates fertile ground for the Spirit to reassure and strengthen our hearts, helping us recall these truths precisely when anxiety arises. Additionally, promptly responding in obedience when the Spirit leads us toward faith, surrender, or specific actions—such as forgiving others, trusting God's timing, or releasing control—actively diminishes anxiety's power. Ultimately, the Holy Spirit transforms anxiety from a burden into an opportunity for deeper trust and intimacy with God, providing us with supernatural peace rooted firmly in his abiding presence.

THE IMPORTANCE OF REST & SABBATH IN REDUCING ANXIETY (EXODUS 20:8–10)

Just as God provided the Holy Spirit to guide us into peace, he also gave us the gift of rest, an essential rhythm established from the very creation of the world. Rest and Sabbath are not merely suggestions; they are foundational elements of God's design for our well-being and crucial tools for reducing anxiety.

In Exodus 20:8–10, we read God's explicit command regarding rest "Remember the Sabbath day by keeping it holy. Six days you shall labor and do all your work, but the seventh day is a Sabbath to the Lord your God. On it you shall not do any work."

This command, rooted in God's own rhythm of creation, highlights the critical importance of intentional rest and renewal. Anxiety often flourishes in lives characterized by relentless busyness, exhaustion, and lack of proper rest. A restless life feeds anxiety, convincing us that everything depends on our constant activity and control.

SABBATH AS A REMEDY FOR ANXIETY

God's command to observe Sabbath rest isn't burdensome; it's liberating. Sabbath rest directly confronts anxiety by teaching us to pause, trusting God to sustain and provide even when we intentionally step away from our efforts.

Sabbath and intentional rest practically help reduce anxiety by teaching us to depend fully on God, providing essential space for renewal, and reinforcing God's goodness and care. Regular rest requires us to trust that God remains sovereignly in control even when we stop striving, countering anxiety's claim that our constant effort is necessary. By deliberately stepping back from busyness, we create opportunities for spiritual, emotional, and physical renewal, allowing our hearts, minds, and bodies to recover through reflection, prayer, and worship. Moreover, Sabbath reminds us of God's compassionate care, demonstrating that he values our wellbeing and peace—not through our continuous efforts, but simply because of his generous and loving nature.

PRACTICAL STEPS TOWARD REST & SABBATH

To find relief from anxiety through Sabbath rest, intentionally create a consistent weekly time dedicated solely to rest, worship, and spiritual renewal. Protect this sacred time, shielding it from unnecessary distractions and obligations. During your Sabbath, engage in activities that restore your soul, such as prayer, meditating on Scripture, connecting with nature, enjoying meaningful time with loved ones, or simply resting deeply.

A key element of Sabbath rest is consciously surrendering control and responsibility. Instead of carrying the weight of unfinished tasks or unresolved worries, actively entrust these concerns to God. Affirm your trust in his sovereignty and ability to work all things for good, allowing yourself to truly rest in his provision. As 1 Peter 5:7 says, "Cast all your anxiety on him because he cares for you."

Furthermore, use your Sabbath time to intentionally reflect on God's goodness, provision, and faithfulness. Worship and gratitude naturally turn our hearts toward confidence and peace, combating anxiety by grounding us in the certainty of God's character. Psalm 46:10 reminds us, "Be still, and know that I am God."

By embracing Sabbath, we align ourselves with God's wise and loving design, experiencing a profound rest that calms anxiety and deepens our trust in his faithful care. Through the empowering presence of the Holy Spirit and the rhythm of Sabbath rest, God offers us powerful and compassionate resources to overcome anxiety, experience genuine peace, and walk confidently in the security of Christ's love.

CHAPTER SUMMARY

This chapter explored the profound truth that lasting peace is rooted in Christ's finished work on the cross—a truth that transforms anxiety into restful trust. Anxiety often stems from uncertainty about God's love and acceptance, tempting us to rely on our own efforts rather than Christ's complete sacrifice. By understanding and anchoring our hearts in the certainty that Jesus fully paid the price for our sins, we find lasting peace, free from guilt, shame, and the relentless pursuit of perfection. We also considered the crucial role of the Holy Spirit in applying this gospel truth, comforting, strengthening, and empowering us to overcome anxiety by reminding us of God's faithful promises. Finally, we explored the importance of Sabbath rest as a God-ordained rhythm to reduce anxiety, fostering dependence on God's sovereign care, providing renewal, and reinforcing his loving character.

HOMEWORK ASSIGNMENTS

Gospel Reflection

This week, set aside 10 to 15 minutes each day to reflect on Christ's powerful declaration from the cross, *"It is finished"* (John 19:30). Let the weight of those words sink into your heart as you consider how complete and secure your acceptance with God truly is. Write a short paragraph each day about how this truth affects your anxiety and shapes your sense of peace. Be honest with your thoughts and notice any shifts in your perspective. At the end of the week, look back over your reflections and summarize how consistently dwelling on Christ's finished work has influenced your overall sense of peace and trust in God.

Inviting the Holy Spirit into Moments of Anxiety

Throughout this week, make it a practice to intentionally invite the Holy Spirit into your moments of anxiety. Pause when you feel anxious and pray, asking the Spirit to guide, comfort, and remind you of biblical truths that counter your fears. Memorize John 14:26–27 and let its promise settle in your heart *"But the Advocate, the Holy Spirit, whom the Father will send in my name, will teach you all things and will remind you of everything I have said to you. Peace I leave with you; my peace I give you."*

Whenever you sense anxiety rising, meditate on these words and record specific instances when you consciously relied on the Spirit's help. At the end of the week, take a few moments to reflect on how inviting the Holy Spirit into your anxiety has impacted your peace and trust in God.

Reflective Questions

1. How does resting in the finished work of Christ change how you respond to stress and anxiety?

2. What practical steps can you take to cultivate a deeper experience of peace through your relationship with Christ?

7

Walking in Faith

Practical Steps to Overcome Anxiety

THE PREVIOUS CHAPTER HIGHLIGHTED how peace is rooted in Christ's finished work, empowered by the Holy Spirit, and nurtured through Sabbath rest. However, freedom from anxiety requires intentional action: actively choosing faith, surrender, and trust. This chapter focuses on practical ways to choose faith over fear, transforming spiritual truths into lived realities.

FAITH AS AN ACTIVE CHOICE
(2 CORINTHIANS 5:7)

Overcoming anxiety involves consistently choosing faith over fear. Anxiety craves control and demands certainty, thriving on the unknown and fueling doubt with questions like, "What if God doesn't come through? What if my worst fears materialize?" God invites us to a different path: "We live by faith, not by sight" (2 Corinthians 5:7).

This verse offers guidance for those struggling with anxiety. Faith isn't passive; it's an active decision to trust God's character, promises, and faithfulness, especially when circumstances are uncertain. Walking by faith means consistently placing our confidence in God's revealed truth, even when emotions and circumstances incline us toward fear or doubt.

Choosing faith means recognizing each moment of anxiety as an opportunity to trust God rather than our own understanding (Proverbs 3:5–6). Anxiety suggests that managing circumstances will eliminate our fears. However, faith acknowledges we can't control everything, nor were we meant to. Instead, faith surrenders control to God, believing that he is wise, good, powerful, and present, even when our feelings suggest otherwise.

Practically, actively choosing faith means identifying anxious thoughts and intentionally countering them with biblical truth. Rather than letting anxiety steer our hearts toward fear, we redirect our thoughts toward God's character and promises. Each time we choose trust over panic; we strengthen our faith and weaken anxiety's grip.

Consider practical examples. When anxiety whispers, "What if I fail?" faith responds, "Even if I stumble, God remains faithful to uphold and guide me" (Psalm 37:23–24). When anxiety suggests, "What if God doesn't provide?" faith reminds us, "My God will meet all my needs according to his glorious riches in Christ Jesus" (Philippians 4:19). When anxiety magnifies loneliness, faith reassures, "Never will he leave me; never will he forsake me" (Hebrews 13:5).

Choosing faith over anxiety demands deliberate practice and consistency. Yet, each time we actively trust God in uncertainty, our faith deepens, and anxiety diminishes. The more we walk by faith, the more we experience God's promised peace—a peace anchored in his unchanging character and unfailing love.

WORSHIP, A POWERFUL TOOL AGAINST ANXIETY

One of the most effective, yet often overlooked, tools against anxiety is worship. At its core, worship redirects our focus from our uncertain circumstances to the unchanging character of God. Anxiety thrives by fixing our eyes on problems, amplifying fears and doubts. Worship, however, lifts our gaze to heaven, reminding us of God's sovereignty, love, faithfulness, and goodness.

Worship is more than singing songs; it's an intentional posture of the heart. It's consciously exalting God above our situations, acknowledging his greatness even amid uncertainty. When anxiety clouds our vision, worship pierces through the fog, anchoring us in God's nature and promises. Psalm 95:6–7 invites us, "Come, let us bow down in worship, let us kneel before the Lord our Maker; for he is our God and we are the people of his pasture, the flock under his care."

Worship disarms anxiety by reorienting our perspective. Where anxiety insists our challenges are insurmountable, worship reminds us that our God is greater. Where anxiety whispers fears about the future, worship declares confidence in God's promises. In worship, anxiety loses its grip as God's power and presence overshadow every fear and doubt.

Practically, worshiping through anxiety means choosing to praise God even when our hearts are heavy. It means singing or reciting truths about God's attributes, even when our emotions lag. It means meditating on Scripture that exalts God, allowing his promises to replace anxious thoughts. Psalm 34:1 models this: "I will extol the Lord at all times; his praise will always be on my lips." This constant praise combats anxiety, transforming fear into faith and worry into peace.

As we consistently worship God, our perspective shifts from problem-centered to God-centered. Anxiety shrinks in the presence of genuine worship because our hearts are anchored in the One who never changes. Worship isn't just a response to God—it's a transformative tool in our daily battle against anxiety.

ENCOURAGEMENT IN THE FIGHT AGAINST ANXIETY (HEBREWS 10:24–25)

God never intended us to face anxiety alone. Anxiety thrives in isolation but weakens within biblical community. Community is God's provision for encouragement, comfort, accountability, and growth. Hebrews 10:24–25 instructs us: "And let us consider how we may spur one another on toward love and good deeds, not giving up meeting together, as some are in the habit of doing, but encouraging one another, and all the more as you see the Day approaching."

These verses highlight the value of supportive relationships within the body of Christ. Anxiety tempts us to withdraw, believing no one understands or that we'll burden others. But withdrawal only deepens distress. Scripture calls us into authentic, vulnerable relationships marked by mutual encouragement.

Biblical community provides a safe space to share anxieties, receiving wisdom, prayer, and comfort from fellow believers who point us to Christ. This community doesn't just sympathize, it actively supports, challenges, and equips us to trust God more deeply. As we gather, pray, and remind each other of God's truths, anxiety's voice diminishes, replaced by hope in Christ.

Practically, this means intentionally seeking relationships where encouragement can flourish. It involves stepping out of isolation, honestly sharing struggles, and allowing others to bear burdens alongside us (Galatians 6:2). In return, we offer compassionate encouragement, strengthening our collective faith.

In biblical community, we experience God's presence through the loving care of other believers. Through fellowship, prayer, accountability, and shared worship, community becomes a source of strength against anxiety. Together, we rehearse God's faithfulness and anchor our hearts in the hope that anxiety cannot overcome.

DAILY DISCIPLINES, SCRIPTURE, JOURNALING, AND GRATITUDE

Overcoming anxiety involves worship and biblical community, but lasting peace is also built through consistent daily disciplines. Anxiety often thrives in unattended spaces, unguarded thoughts, unchecked worries, or neglected spiritual habits. Intentional practices like scripture reading, journaling, and cultivating gratitude protect our hearts and minds, guiding us toward steady peace.

SCRIPTURE, ANCHORING IN TRUTH

Daily engagement with scripture is essential because anxiety distorts reality, amplifies fears, and pushes us toward despair. God's Word counteracts these distortions by anchoring us in divine truth. Hebrews 4:12 reminds us, "For the word of God is alive and active. . . it judges the thoughts and attitudes of the heart." Scripture penetrates anxious thoughts, exposing lies and replacing them with God's promises and character.

Regular Bible reading equips us to face anxiety proactively. Immersing ourselves in scripture daily builds a reservoir of truth, accessible when anxiety strikes. Internalized verses come to mind, providing comfort, reassurance, and strength. When anxiety whispers of inadequacy, scripture reminds us, "My grace is sufficient for you, for my power is made perfect in weakness" (2 Corinthians 12:9). Consistent reading transforms our hearts, teaching us to respond with faith instead of fear.

GRATITUDE

Cultivating gratitude is essential. Anxiety often magnifies what we lack or what might go wrong. Gratitude redirects our perspective toward God's goodness, provision, and faithfulness. It reminds us that God's blessings consistently outweigh our struggles, even when challenges are significant.

Practicing gratitude is transformative, shifting our focus from worries to tangible evidence of God's care. Paul encourages this in 1 Thessalonians 5:18 "Give thanks in all circumstances; for this is God's will for you in Christ Jesus." Gratitude becomes a daily choice, a habit of recognizing and celebrating God's abundant grace.

INTEGRATING DAILY DISCIPLINES

To integrate these disciplines, set aside dedicated time each day, perhaps in the morning or before bed. Immerse yourself in scripture, allowing God's truth to shape your thoughts. Follow this with journaling, honestly reflecting on your worries, God's presence, and how he is working in your life. Lastly, spend time giving thanks, naming specific ways God has been faithful.

Together, these practices form a foundation of spiritual health that combats anxiety. Scripture provides truth, journaling offers clarity and remembrance, and gratitude cultivates joy and trust. As we faithfully pursue these disciplines, anxiety's grip weakens, replaced by growing confidence and enduring peace rooted in God's love.

RELATIONAL AND CHURCH COMMUNITY INTEGRATION

Anxiety can feel like a personal battle, but we are called to face it within a supportive community. God designed His people to walk alongside one another, sharing burdens and offering encouragement. The church is meant to be a refuge, a place where believers find strength and support in a faith community.

Scripture encourages us to "bear one another's burdens, and so fulfill the law of Christ" (Galatians 6:2). Fighting anxiety isn't a solitary task but a shared journey within the body of Christ. When we share our struggles, we allow others to support us through prayer and encouragement. James reminds us, "Confess your sins to each other and pray for each other so that you may be healed" (James 5:16). Letting others walk with us brings healing and hope as they speak truth in love (Ephesians 4:15) and remind us of God's faithfulness.

Don't face anxiety alone. Seek fellow believers who will pray for you, support you, and remind you of God's promises. Let the church be a place where you find refuge, encouragement, and a deeper understanding of God's presence through the love and care of others.

CHAPTER SUMMARY

Overcoming anxiety requires an active choice, not a passive approach. It involves intentionally choosing faith over fear through consistent worship, supportive community, and daily spiritual practices. Walking by faith means deliberately trusting God's character and promises, especially when anxiety tempts us toward fear or doubt. Worship redirects our focus from overwhelming circumstances to God's unchanging nature, powerfully combating anxiety's grip. Biblical community breaks isolation, allowing us to receive and offer encouragement, prayer, and support, reinforcing faith and diminishing anxiety's power. Daily disciplines, like Scripture reading, journaling, and gratitude, anchor our minds in God's truth, help us process anxieties openly before him, and shift our focus toward his abundant blessings. These practical steps build a resilient spiritual foundation, continually guiding our hearts away from anxiety and toward lasting peace in Christ.

HOMEWORK ASSIGNMENTS

Choosing Faith Actively

This week make it a priority to notice specific anxious thoughts that tend to surface in your mind. As each thought arises, pause and seek out at least one biblical truth or promise that directly counters it. Write these truths down and intentionally practice replacing the anxious thoughts with them each day. At the end of each day, take a few moments to reflect and journal about how this practice has impacted your anxiety and strengthened your faith. Be honest about the challenges and the progress you observe as you actively choose faith over fear.

Worship as a Tool

Whenever you feel anxiety beginning to rise, intentionally choose worship as your response. Set aside times this week to immerse yourself in worship, whether through singing, listening to music, or reading worshipful Psalms. Consider creating a worship playlist filled with songs or hymns that declare God's sovereignty, faithfulness, and goodness. Make it a habit to turn to worship whenever anxiety creeps in, allowing the truth of God's character to reframe your perspective. At the end of the week, spend some time journaling about how worshiping God has impacted your outlook, emotional state, and ability to trust him amid anxious moments.

Reflective Questions

1. How can active faith change your perspective on daily challenges that trigger anxiety?

2. What role does biblical community play in helping you overcome anxiety, and how can you invite others into your journey?

8

Trusting God for the Journey

As we reach the end of our time together in this book, please know this, you are deeply loved and never alone in your struggle with anxiety. We've explored anxiety through God's compassionate heart, examining its roots, correcting misunderstandings about his nature, and discovering lasting peace in Christ. We've discussed the power and freedom found in Jesus' finished work, the Holy Spirit's guidance, and the strength found in daily spiritual practices.

Moving forward, you might still fear the return of anxiety or feel your progress is undone. Please hear this, setbacks don't mean you've failed, nor do they lessen God's love for you. In this final chapter, I offer encouragement and assurance, reminding you of God's faithfulness as you continue to trust him.

I understand how painful setbacks can be, when anxiety returns unexpectedly, making you question if change is possible. These moments can feel overwhelming, exhausting, or even shameful. But setbacks don't reflect your worth, strength, or faithfulness. They remind us of our human condition in a broken world.

God's Word acknowledges this, offering comfort. Proverbs 24:16 reminds us, "For though the righteous fall seven times, they rise again." God focuses on our rising, not our falling. Each time anxiety returns, it's an opportunity to lean into God's grace. Our goal is growing dependence on the Lord who holds us, especially when anxiety returns.

Remember, biblical figures faced anxiety and setbacks. David experienced fear, yet he poured his heart out to God, who met him with compassion (Psalm 56:3–4). Elijah battled anxiety and despair, yet God restored him (1 Kings 19). Peter stumbled, yet Jesus restored him (John 21). Scripture shares these stories to comfort and encourage us. God's mercies are new each morning (Lamentations 3:22–23), meeting us in our need.

When anxiety returns, don't despair. See it as an invitation to draw nearer to Jesus, resting in his love. Your peace depends on his faithfulness, not your consistency.

Perseverance is important, but it doesn't rely on your strength alone. Hebrews 12:1 urges us to "run with perseverance the race marked out for us, fixing our eyes on Jesus, the pioneer and perfecter of faith." Perseverance comes as we fix our gaze on Christ, resting in his faithful presence.

When anxiety feels overwhelming, remember that God hasn't abandoned you. He continues to write your story, holding your heart gently. Philippians 1:6 promises "he who began a good work in you will carry it on to completion until the day of Christ Jesus." Your journey toward peace is a work God promises to complete. Trust him to carry you through each moment, thought, and day.

Perseverance means bringing every anxious thought to your Heavenly Father, who welcomes you as you are. This journey involves returning to his grace, laying down anxieties, and choosing obedience, even on difficult days. Each step in trust roots you in God's love, transforming your heart with his peace.

CLOSING PRAYER

Heavenly Father, I come before you with gratitude for your unfailing love, sovereign care, and unending grace and mercy. Thank you for walking with me through every anxious moment and for revealing the truth in your word that anchors me in who you are as Almighty God. I acknowledge my continual dependence on you and confess that I cannot overcome anxiety in my strength alone. Lord, when anxiety returns, remind me of your faithfulness, your promises, and your abiding presence.

Give me courage to persevere when setbacks come, and strength to keep trusting you, even when the road is difficult. Let my heart rest securely in Jesus' finished work and empower me daily through the presence and power of the Holy Spirit.

I surrender every anxious thought to your sovereign control, asking that you use each struggle to deepen my faith and trust in you. Equip me to be an encouragement to others battling anxiety, allowing my experiences to reflect your love, patience, and grace.

As I move forward, may my life be a testimony of your love, grace and peace, a peace that surpasses understanding, rooted firmly in your word and who you are as God.

In Jesus' name, Amen.

Afterword

IN THE GENTLE, HESITANT light of morning, Rebecca sat at her kitchen table, the familiar wood feeling cold beneath her trembling hands. She lifted her mug, taking a slow sip of coffee that had long turned cold, barely registering the bitter taste. Her mind was far away, restlessly retracing the steps of a sleepless night.

Rebecca's eyes were tired, shadowed by hours of worry. It began with a simple mistake, a misstep at work that she now replayed over and over. The more she dwelled on it, the larger it seemed, growing into something far more burdensome than the initial error.

Each anxious thought crashed against her mind like a relentless wave, whispering all the ways things could go wrong. What if her boss couldn't understand? What if they decided she wasn't good enough? What if losing this job meant losing everything she had struggled to achieve? The questions swirled endlessly, their constant murmurs leaving her breathless, as if the very air had become too thin to breathe.

She gently placed the mug back on the table, her fingers still trembling, and rubbed her temples, longing for some relief. But the anxiety clung tightly, refusing to loosen its grip, leaving Rebecca feeling utterly alone and trapped within her own thoughts. In these quiet, vulnerable moments, her heart ached deeply, not only from worry but from a quiet yearning for peace, for rest, or simply for the reassurance that she wasn't the only one who felt this way.

Even as the sun climbed higher, sending delicate streams of light through her kitchen window, Rebecca felt little of its warmth. The weight remained heavy, silent, and ever-present.

Rebecca felt that familiar dread creeping in, a heavy weight threatening to pull her under. Desperate for a lifeline, she reached for her phone and began scrolling through social media. Bright photos and smiling faces flashed across the screen, but they didn't register, their manufactured cheerfulness only amplifying the emptiness inside. Articles promising wellness and motivation just made her feel even more inadequate. She knew she should put the phone down, that it wasn't helping, but distraction felt like the only shield against the rising tide of anxious thoughts.

Finally, she tossed the phone onto the table, the screen going dark as if surrendering. Trying to release the tension coiled tight in her body, she started scrubbing the kitchen counters, wiping the same spot over and over. Soft, calming music drifted from her laptop, but the rhythm of the cloth against the surface only echoed the frantic beating of her heart. The music, intended to soothe, felt distant, disconnected from the turmoil she was experiencing.

Her mind wouldn't quiet. Every detail of yesterday's mistake at work replayed endlessly. Rebecca could still picture her boss's concerned expression, hear the slight edge in his voice when he asked her to correct the problem. Was he disappointed? Frustrated? Upset? The faces of her co-workers seemed different now, in her memory. Had they noticed? Were they talking about her behind her back? With each repetition of these thoughts, Rebecca's anxiety tightened its grip, suffocating her with imagined possibilities.

By the time she forced herself to go to work, she was drained, her nerves stretched thin. As she sat down at her desk, Mallory appeared, offering a kind smile. "Hey, are you okay? You seem a little out of sorts."

The question felt like an accusation, a spotlight suddenly shining on her. A wave of defensiveness washed over Rebecca before she could stop it. "I'm fine," she snapped, the words sharper than she meant them to be. The look on Mallory's face, a mix of hurt and confusion, sent a pang of guilt through Rebecca.

"Okay," Mallory replied quietly, stepping back. "Just checking in." She hesitated, as if hoping Rebecca would say more, but when she didn't, Mallory turned and walked away, her shoulders slightly slumped.

Regret settled heavily in Rebecca's stomach, a cold stone. Now, guilt piled on top of the anxiety, an unbearable weight. She had pushed away someone who was trying to help. Alone at her desk, Rebecca stared at her computer screen, but the words swam before her eyes, refusing to make sense. In that moment, the combined weight of her fear, guilt, and isolation felt crushing, almost too much to bear.

The rest of the workday seemed to drag on forever, each minute feeling longer than the one before. Rebecca did her best to stay quiet, barely speaking to anyone. She worried that if she opened her mouth, the anxiety swirling inside her would spill out. She saw Mallory moving around the office, but didn't dare go near her. The guilt was eating away at her, but the thought of admitting how anxious she felt was too much, too exposing.

When the workday finally ended, Rebecca drove home in silence, her mind stuck on the tension with Mallory that morning. The moment she walked into her apartment, the quiet seemed to amplify her worries. She dropped her keys on the counter and sank onto the worn sofa, rubbing her temples as a headache threatened to take hold.

Desperate for a little comfort, she reached for her phone and called her mom. Her mother answered quickly, her voice full of warmth.

"Hey, sweetie! How was your day?"

Rebecca hesitated; her voice shaky. "Not great," she managed to say. "I made a mistake at work yesterday, and I can't stop thinking about it. I'm worried it might get me fired, and I just. . . I don't know what to do."

There was a pause. Then her mom's voice softened, but stayed practical, as if she was trying to talk Rebecca out of her fear. "Honey, just relax. You're overthinking things. Everyone makes mistakes. You're making a big deal out of nothing. Stop worrying so much."

Rebecca bit her lip, trying not to cry. She knew her mom meant well, but her words didn't help. They felt like a quick fix for something much deeper. Just relax. If only it were that easy. A heavy feeling settled in her chest, and she forced herself to sound grateful. "Yeah, you're probably right. Thanks, Mom."

After she hung up, the quiet felt even louder. Rebecca's hands trembled as she tried to distract herself, reorganizing the mail, tidying the living room. But her thoughts kept coming back, like a relentless wave. She tried the breathing exercises she'd read about online, counting to four as she breathed in, holding it, then slowly breathing out. But instead of calming her, it made her focus on her racing heart, each beat pounding in her ears. She felt frustrated, and her stomach tightened.

As evening turned to night, Rebecca found herself reaching for her Bible, hoping for something to give her relief. She flipped through the pages, looking for comfort, but the words seemed blurry, unable to break through her panic. It felt like trying to see something beautiful through a foggy window, there, but out of reach.

She set the Bible down and sighed, covering her face with her hands. "God, why can't I feel you? Why can't I just be okay? Why am I like this?" The silence that followed felt heavy, pressing down on her. Feeling completely exhausted, she curled up on the couch, her chest tight with fear, guilt, and frustration. Peace felt distant, out of reach, and slipping further away with every breath.

The hours drifted by shadows stretching long and thick as night enveloped the apartment. Rebecca hardly noticed the deepening darkness, her mind overwhelmed by the anxious storm within. She remained still on the couch, her phone lying forgotten beside her. She lacked the energy to respond to Mallory's earlier, concerned text. The ache in her chest hadn't lessened; instead, it had grown stronger, tightening like a constricting cord.

She desperately hoped for a breakthrough, a moment of clarity, a comforting thought, anything to make sense of the chaos swirling in her head. But nothing came. The silence of the room seemed to mock her, highlighting how utterly alone she felt in this struggle. Restless, she pulled the worn throw blanket tighter around her and stared blankly at the wall, willing her mind to quiet, but it wouldn't obey. The same troubling thoughts circled endlessly, becoming more tangled with each repetition.

Eventually, the tension became unbearable, and a sob escaped her throat. She buried her face in her hands, unable to hold back the tears any longer. They streamed down her face, soaking her palms as she whispered a prayer, more of a desperate plea than a coherent request.

"God, I just want this to end. Why can't I feel normal? Why can't I trust you like others seem to? I'm so tired of feeling this way . . . I just need it to stop. Please, just make it stop . . ."

She waited, her breathing uneven, longing for some relief or comfort, a gentle whisper to calm the storm within. But the room remained suffocatingly still, her cries absorbed into the silence. Nothing changed. No peace descended upon her; no reassuring presence appeared. Only the weight of her own pain pressed against her.

Wiping her tear-streaked cheeks, Rebecca let out a shaky breath, feeling more defeated than ever. She couldn't escape the guilt for not being stronger, for not trusting more fully, for feeling so spiritually inadequate. Deep down, she wondered if she was failing in her faith altogether. What kind of Christian couldn't even believe that God would care for her?

Finally, exhaustion overcame her, and she collapsed onto the couch, her eyes heavy and sore, her heart still racing. As sleep began to claim her, the questions remained unanswered, and the ache in her soul remained.

The morning light, pale and thin, seeped through the curtains, gently nudging Rebecca awake. She blinked at the ceiling, the familiar weight pressing on her chest, a reminder that the night hadn't magically erased her struggles. Her body ached from a restless sleep on the couch, and her mind was already swirling with familiar worries. She released a long, shaky breath, attempting to gather the strength for another day, but the thought of work brought a familiar knot to her stomach.

Slowly, she sat up, pushing tangled hair away from her face. The emptiness inside felt almost heavier than the anxiety itself, a deep, hollow ache that offered no relief. She moved through her morning routine almost without thinking, brushing her teeth and pulling on a sweater, trying to quiet the nagging voice whispering that today would be a repeat of yesterday. That nothing would improve.

At work, the office buzzed with the usual sounds keyboards clicking, phones ringing, voices blending into a soft hum. Rebecca quietly slipped into her seat, hoping to fade into the background. She focused on her screen, doing her best to appear busy, but her thoughts kept drifting, caught in the same cycle of doubt and fear.

After a while, Mallory approached, her presence gentle, as if approaching someone fragile. Rebecca looked up, managing a weak smile that didn't quite reach her eyes. Mallory hesitated before speaking, her voice soft and careful.

"Hey . . . are you okay?" she asked, her worry was evident.

Rebecca swallowed hard, fighting the urge to dismiss it with a hollow "I'm fine." Instead, the truth slipped out, her voice barely audible. "Not really," she admitted, her gaze dropping to the desk. "Just . . . having a tough time."

Mallory nodded, her concern deepening, but she didn't push for details. She simply stayed there, offering quiet support without adding pressure. Rebecca appreciated this unspoken kindness, but the shame still lingered shame for feeling so overwhelmed, so broken, so unable to simply cope.

When Mallory finally stepped away, giving her space, Rebecca felt a pang of guilt for not being more open, for not trusting her friend with her full feelings. But the fear of judgment or pity kept her guarded, the vulnerability too tender to reveal.

As lunchtime arrived, Rebecca found herself sitting alone by the window, her food untouched before her. She gazed out at the street below, watching cars and people moving with purpose. She wished she could step into their lives, even briefly, to experience something other than this aching emptiness. Her mind kept returning to the same thoughts, circling endlessly without finding a solution. Trapped. That's how she felt trapped in this relentless cycle of anxiety and despair, unsure how to escape.

She closed her eyes, resting her forehead against the cool glass, and let out a slow, trembling breath. The world continued around her, unaware of the quiet storm raging inside.

Questions

1. If Rebecca was your friend, how would you counsel her from a biblical perspective?

2. How could you help her understand the spiritual roots of her anxiety and guide her to find true peace in Christ?

3. What Scriptures would you encourage her to meditate on, and why?

4. How would you approach helping her establish practical, faith-based habits to combat anxiety?

5. How could the faith community play a role in supporting Rebecca as she works through her struggles?

Appendix 1

Theological Glossary

Anxiety (Biblical): A response of the heart reflecting fear, worry, or lack of trust in God's care, sovereignty, or provision. While anxiety can stem from physical or situational causes, Scripture treats it as both a spiritual burden and an invitation to trust God more deeply (Philippians 4:6–7; Matthew 6:25–34).

Aseity: God's self-existence and independence from all creation. He is the source of all life and sustains all things. This attribute reminds us that God lacks nothing and depends on no one, making him fully trustworthy and sufficient (Exodus 3:14; John 5:26).

Atonement: The reconciling work of Christ who bore God's wrath and paid the penalty for sin on the cross. Through his atoning sacrifice, believers are forgiven and restored to right relationship with God (Isaiah 53:5; Romans 3:25).

Common Grace: God's kindness shown to all humanity, regardless of salvation. This includes provision, restraint of evil, beauty in creation, and societal order (Matthew 5:45).

Faithfulness of God: God is always true to his promises, character, and word. He is unwavering and dependable in every circumstance (Lamentations 3:22–23; 2 Timothy 2:13).

God's Sovereignty: God's complete authority and rule over all things. He governs the universe with wisdom and purpose, ensuring that nothing escapes his control—even our suffering or anxious thoughts (Isaiah 46:9–10; Romans 8:28).

Goodness of God: God is the source and standard of all that is good. His actions are always benevolent, kind, and aimed at the flourishing of his creation—even when discipline or trials are involved (Psalm 119:68; Nahum 1:7).

Grace of God: God's unearned favor toward undeserving sinners. Grace includes forgiveness, strength for daily living, and the hope of eternal life. It assures us that God's help is always available, not earned (Ephesians 2:8–9; Titus 2:11–12).

Holiness of God: God's complete purity and moral perfection. He is set apart from sin and calls his people to reflect his holiness. His holiness is not distant but relational, inviting us into transformation (Isaiah 6:3; 1 Peter 1:15–16).

Imago Dei (Image of God): The biblical truth that all humans are created in God's image (Genesis 1:27), which gives every person value, dignity, and moral responsibility. Though marred by sin, this image is being restored in Christ (Colossians 3:10).

Immutability of God: God does not change in his being, purposes, or promises. He is the same yesterday, today, and forever (Malachi 3:6; Hebrews 13:8).

Justification: God's legal declaration that a sinner is righteous based on the finished work of Christ. This verdict is granted through faith and not based on human performance (Romans 5:1; 2 Corinthians 5:21).

Love of God: God's benevolent affection and self-giving for the good of his people. His love is sacrificial, eternal, and unbreakable (Romans 5:8; Romans 8:38–39).

Omnipresence of God: God is present everywhere at all times. For the anxious soul, this means you are never alone—God is always near to help (Psalm 139:7–10; Jeremiah 23:23–24).

Omnipotence of God: God is all-powerful, able to do all his holy will. His strength is perfect in our weakness (Jeremiah 32:17; 2 Corinthians 12:9–10).

Omniscience of God: God knows all things—past, present, and future. He understands our fears and thoughts before we speak them (Psalm 147:5; Hebrews 4:13).

Providence: God's ongoing care and guidance over creation and human history. He works all things according to his will, including the details of our daily lives (Proverbs 16:9; Psalm 103:19).

Redemptive Suffering: God uses suffering in the lives of believers to grow faith, produce endurance, and conform us to Christ. In his hands, suffering is never wasted (Romans 5:3–5; 2 Corinthians 4:16–18).

Salvation: God's complete work in Jesus of rescuing sinners from sin's penalty, power, and ultimately, death. It includes justification, sanctification, and glorification, secured by grace through faith (Ephesians 2:8–9; John 10:28–29).

Sanctification: The ongoing work of the Holy Spirit transforming believers into the image of Christ. This lifelong process involves resisting sin and growing in holiness (1 Thessalonians 4:3; Romans 12:1–2).

Scripture (Biblical Authority and Sufficiency): The inspired, inerrant, and authoritative Word of God, sufficient for all life, faith, and godliness (2 Timothy 3:16–17; Psalm 19:7–11).

Trust (Biblical Faith): More than intellectual belief—faith is relational reliance on God's character and promises, demonstrated by obedience even in uncertainty (Proverbs 3:5–6; Hebrews 11:6).

Union with Christ: The spiritual reality that believers are united with Jesus in his life, death, and resurrection. Through this union, we receive all spiritual blessings (John 15:4–5; Ephesians 1:3–14).

Appendix 2

Daily Scripture Declarations Rooted in God's Character

Two Weeks of Biblical Promises for the Anxious Heart

WEEK ONE: GOD'S UNFAILING LOVE AND COMPASSION

Day 1—God's Love Never Fails

"Give thanks to the Lord, for he is good; his love endures forever." Psalm 136:1

Declaration: God's love for me never ends, and I am secure in his steadfast care.

Day 2—God's Love Is Perfect

"There is no fear in love. But perfect love drives out fear." 1 John 4:18

Declaration: God's perfect love frees me from fear and fills me with peace.

Day 3—God's Love Is Unchanging

"Though the mountains be shaken and the hills be removed, yet my unfailing love for you will not be shaken." Isaiah 54:10

Declaration: Even when life feels unstable, God's love remains constant and unmovable.

Day 4—God's Compassion Is Unfailing

"Because of the Lord's great love we are not consumed, for his compassions never fail." Lamentations 3:22

Declaration: God's compassion sustains me when I am overwhelmed, and is mercy renews my strength.

Day 5—God's Love Is Personal

"The Lord your God is with you, the Mighty Warrior who saves. He will take great delight in you; in his love he will no longer rebuke you, but will rejoice over you with singing." Zephaniah 3:17

Declaration: God delights in me and surrounds me with his joyful love.

Day 6—God's Love Is Sacrificial

"But God demonstrates his own love for us in this: While we were still sinners, Christ died for us." Romans 5:8

Declaration: God proved his love through the sacrifice of his Son, and I am deeply loved and forgiven.

Day 7—God's Love Comforts

"I will not leave you as orphans; I will come to you."—John 14:18

Declaration: God's love surrounds me, and I am never abandoned or forgotten.

WEEK TWO: GOD'S MERCY AND GRACE

Day 8—God's Grace Is Sufficient

"But he said to me, 'My grace is sufficient for you, for my power is made perfect in weakness.'" 2 Corinthians 12:9

Declaration: God's grace meets me in my weakness and empowers me to endure.

Day 9—God's Mercy Is New Every Morning

"The steadfast love of the Lord never ceases; his mercies never come to an end; they are new every morning." Lamentations 3:22–23

Declaration: Every day, God's mercy renews my spirit and gives me hope.

Day 10—God Is Rich in Mercy

"But because of his great love for us, God, who is rich in mercy, made us alive with Christ." Ephesians 2:4–5

Declaration: God's mercy breathes life into my soul and awakens me to his grace.

Day 11—God's Grace Covers All My Sin

"In him we have redemption through his blood, the forgiveness of sins, in accordance with the riches of God's grace." Ephesians 1:7

Declaration: I am forgiven and redeemed by the richness of God's grace through Christ.

Day 12—God's Mercy Leads to Repentance

"Or do you show contempt for the riches of his kindness, forbearance and patience, not realizing that God's kindness is intended to lead you to repentance?" Romans 2:4

Declaration: God's kindness and mercy draw me closer to him in repentance and renewal.

Day 13—God Is Full of Grace and Truth

"The Word became flesh and made his dwelling among us. We have seen his glory, the glory of the one and only Son, who came from the Father, full of grace and truth." John 1:14

Declaration: Jesus embodies grace and truth, and I receive his fullness as I follow Jesus.

Day 14—God's Mercy Triumphs Over Judgment

"Because judgment without mercy will be shown to anyone who has not been merciful. Mercy triumphs over judgment." James 2:13

Declaration: In Christ, mercy has triumphed over judgment, and I am covered by his grace.

Appendix 3

Ten Psalms for the Anxious Heart

Using the "Turn, Trust, Talk" Model
to Pray Through Psalms

THE PSALMS GIVE VOICE to the deepest longings and fears of the human heart. In seasons of anxiety, they invite us to turn to God, trust his promises, and talk honestly about our struggles. This simple model—*Turn, Trust, Talk*—guides how we approach each psalm:

1. **Turn:** Turn your attention to God, acknowledging His presence and His power.

2. **Trust:** Meditate on His promises and let them shape your heart and mind.

3. **Talk:** Honestly share your thoughts and feelings with Him, holding nothing back.

Here are ten Psalms specifically chosen for anxious hearts, categorized by common struggles.

FEAR OF THE FUTURE

When fear grips your heart and you feel overwhelmed by what lies ahead.

Psalm 27:1–3

Turn: Acknowledge God as your light and salvation, the stronghold of your life.

Trust: Confess that even when enemies surround you, your heart will not fear.

Talk: Share your anxieties about the future and ask for God's peace.

Psalm 46:1–3

Turn: Recognize God as your refuge and strength, an ever-present help in trouble.

Trust: Rest in the assurance that God is with you, even if the world around you shakes.

Talk: Confess your fear and ask God to strengthen your trust.

SLEEPLESSNESS

When anxious thoughts rob you of rest and keep you awake at night.

Psalm 4:8

Turn: Remember that God alone makes you dwell in safety.

Trust: Claim His promise of peaceful sleep despite your anxious mind.

Talk: Pour out your restless thoughts and ask for His calming presence.

Psalm 121:3–4

Turn: Lift your eyes to the One who never slumbers or sleeps.

Trust: Rest in knowing that God is constantly watching over you.

Talk: Share the burdens that keep you awake and ask for His watchful care.

GUILT

When shame and regret weigh heavy on your soul.

Psalm 32:1–5

Turn: Come before God honestly, acknowledging your need for forgiveness.

Trust: Receive His promise of cleansing and freedom.

Talk: Confess your guilt openly and thank Him for the joy of forgiveness.

Psalm 51:10–12

Turn: Seek God's mercy and a clean heart.

Trust: Trust that He can renew your spirit and restore your joy.

Talk: Speak openly about your failures and ask for restoration.

LONELINESS

When you feel isolated, abandoned, or unseen.

Psalm 25:16–18

Turn: Seek God's presence and His understanding of your pain.

Trust: Remember that He sees your distress and forgives your sins.

Talk: Share your loneliness and ask for His companionship.

Psalm 34:18

Turn: Embrace God's nearness to the brokenhearted.

Trust: Rest in the truth that He saves those crushed in spirit.

Talk: Pour out your heart and ask for His comforting touch.

WAITING

When anxiety builds as you wait for answers or change.

Psalm 27:13–14

Turn: Set your hope on seeing God's goodness in the land of the living.

Trust: Wait for the Lord with a strong and courageous heart.

Talk: Express your impatience and ask for strength to trust His timing.

Psalm 130:5–6

Turn: Declare your hope in His Word while you wait.

Trust: Lean on His promise that those who wait on the Lord will not be disappointed.

Talk: Speak honestly about your frustrations and ask for steadfast faith.

ENCOURAGEMENT

Praying the Psalms is an invitation to honest conversation with God, not just reciting words. Let the Psalms guide you to share your burdens, listen for his voice, and find peace in his promises. God's Word provides a safe place to turn, trust, and talk, no matter if you are facing fear, restlessness, guilt, loneliness, or anxious waiting.

May these Psalms draw you nearer to God and remind you that you are always accompanied in your difficulties. He hears you, he cares for you, and he will faithfully meet you where you are.

Bibliography

Bridges, Jerry. *Trusting God: Even When Life Hurts*. NavPress, 1988.

Dillow, Linda. *Calm My Anxious Heart: A Woman's Guide to Finding Contentment*. NavPress, 1998.

Lucado, Max. *Anxious for Nothing: Finding Calm in a Chaotic World*. Thomas Nelson, 2017.

Welch, Edward T. *Running Scared: Fear, Worry, and the God of Rest*. New Growth Press, 2007.

Welch, Edward T. *When People Are Big and God Is Small: Overcoming Peer Pressure, Codependency, and the Fear of Man*. P&R Publishing, 1997.